DIAPERS TO DORMS

Raising kids you actually like, who others like,
and who like themselves

RANDY PARDUE

Published by Author Academy Elite
P.O. Box 43, Powell OH 43065 (USA)
www.AuthorAcademyElite.com

Library of Congress control number: 2018907733

Softcover ISBN: 978-1-64085-354-6
Hardcover ISBN: 978-1-64085-355-3
eBook ISBN: 978-1-64085-356-0

To my kids; Jarod, Abby, Eric, and Jackson for being patient with me as I sought to be a good and loving parent.

To Tammy, who has always been the better parent, and who inspires me to pursue my dreams of writing.

CONTENTS

PROLOGUE

It was late October in the foothills of the Appalachian Mountains. I had been away for a weekend expedition of climbing and rappelling with a team of high school students. I was laying on the floor of our living room because I had wrenched my back helping a fearful student climb up beyond the crevice. My wife, Tammy, came in with our little tribe, Jarod Austin, who had just turned three years old in late summer, and Abigail Layne, our princess, barely six months old.

I looked at the three of them, and my thoughts were flooded with the reality that I had the perfect family. Tammy and I met in high school and married a couple of years after we graduated. We had been married just shy of a year and a half when she walked into the room where I was ironing my clothes. It was at that moment; I found out I would be a dad. We spent the next few months setting up a baby room, buying a Jenny Lind baby bed, and gearing up for a changed life. In those days, no one had heard of a baby reveal party. You simply showed up at the hospital and found out what it was when the baby popped out. It was a boy! Life was good.

Jarod was a just a little over two years old when we loaded up the van and headed to Vail, Colorado for a holiday. We had a couple of friends who had moved out there earlier in the year to begin a church. One morning, while we were getting ready for a day of adventure in the Rockies, Tammy felt a little nauseous. We assumed it was the change in altitude. After a few days of this sporadic nausea, we realized that we were expecting a second child! We were surprised but excited.

Parent life was amazing. We moved that Jenny Lind bed out of Jarod's room, and we painted a twin bed that belonged to my grandmother and set it up in his room. We set that Jenny Lind up and made Abby's room fit for a princess.

So, as I was laying there in the floor, Tammy walked up holding Abby on her hip, like only a mother can do, as Jarod plopped down next to me on the floor. My bride looked at me and asked, "Are you still feeling pretty bad?" I said, "yeah baby." Thinking to myself, *what a caring, thoughtful wife God had blessed me with.* Then she looked at me and said, "I can make you feel worse." In shock at her response, I looked up at her with a slightly puzzled look, and then, I saw it. It was that look I had seen before. The one that says, "We're pregnant . . . again!"

So, two days after our sixth anniversary, we had three kids under the age of four. Eric Daniel had been added to the family, and we were now *really* parenting. I mean, we were outnumbered! A gracious friend gave us a twin stroller. It was not one of the side-by-side models of today; it was one seat forward facing and one seat rear facing. We put Abby and Eric in the seats and made Jarod stand on the axle. It was the only way to keep control.

It wasn't long before we adapted to the larger family. Parenting was fun, and we were loving life. We stored that Jenny Lind baby bed in the attic and put an antique iron bed for the princess and some crate bunk beds for the boys.

One night, when Tammy and I were nearing the forty-year-old mark, we were lying in bed chatting about life. We talked about how good it was, how our little family was getting big, and how awesome our little farmhouse was. At some point in the conversation, she said, "We are getting older, we ought to do something so we don't get pregnant." I laughed. "Come on! One of us is broken. For thirteen years we've not used any birth control, and we aren't pregnant. Relax."

The next month, Tammy had that familiar nauseous feeling. She made an appointment to see the doctor. I couldn't go with her because I had a pre-marital counseling appointment with a young couple. I don't even remember what I said during that meeting. All I could think about was Tammy and whether we were pregnant or not. I walked into that doctor's office, looked at Tammy wearing her red checkered sundress, and the look on the nurse's face. I knew. I was going to be a dad . . . again!

After the initial shock wore off, we felt a tinge of embarrassment at what our kids, who were seventeen, fourteen, and thirteen years old at the time, would think about their parents being pregnant. What a relief it was to realize that they were excited.

In the spring of that year, we pulled out the Jenny Lind baby bed and settled into the realization that we were starting over . . . again! By the time Jackson Lee was a year and a half old, we had one in college and one still in diapers.

We were experiencing what few parents ever experience . . . a mulligan . . . a do-over . . . a second chance. At the time of this writing, Jackson is in college. We have four grown adults. We survived! We literally had one in diapers and one in a dorm, hence the title of this book, *Diapers to Dorms*.

Three of our kids are married now. We have nine grandkids, six boys and three girls. When our oldest grandson, William Cole, was three months old, his mom (our daughter) and her husband moved to Birmingham to start life after college. They moved in with us while they were looking for a home. We pulled out that old Jenny Lind baby bed.

A few years ago, they decided to renovate an old farmhouse, so they moved in with us again. At that time, Cole was nine years old, his little brothers were seven and six, and his sister was four. We pulled out that old twin bed of my grandmothers, and we set up the old bunk beds. They lived with us for almost a year. In a sense, we had an opportunity for a third do-over. We learned a lot that year as we watched, first hand, our daughter and son-in-law raise their kids. It's different as a grandparent, but that's another story altogether.

My oldest child gave us our first granddaughter almost eight years ago. Harper Kate was born with about four different brain abnormalities. As a result, she doesn't walk or talk and has to eat with a feeding tube. But these challenges haven't kept her from having an incredible impact on all that meet her. She has a wit about her that is so like her dad, and she has a smile that I would walk the world to see. She is the Princess of Peachtree. She is our typical, non-typical. But, again, she's another story altogether.

All of that to say, we find ourselves in a unique situation. If you are reading this book and have kids at home, well . . . so do we. If you have grown kids, well . . . so do we. If you are grandparents, well . . . so are we! You have a special needs child, well . . . so do we. What this means for you, the reader is; we can relate to whatever stage of child-rearing you find yourself in. We can't wait to share with you all that we have learned in our time of parenting and grandparenting. So, sit back, grab something to drink, flip the pages, and let's help you raise kids that you like to be with, who others like to be with, and who ultimately like themselves!

PART ONE

GETTING A HEALTHY AND REALISTIC PARENT MINDSET

This book helps you sift through your own life and develop a healthy mindset for parenting successfully. You will most likely change more than your kids will change.

CHAPTER ONE

STEPPING IN THE "RIGHT DIRECTION" BEATS "GOOD INTENTIONS"

Why "intending" to be a good parent isn't enough

I've been a DIY guy most of my life. When Tammy and I bought our first home, it needed a little work. We wanted a few walls taken out, old hardwood floors refinished, a bathroom updated, a new deck, and we wanted to replace the AC window unit with central air. In those days, you didn't just YouTube it, or Google it; you actually had to either get an experienced person to help, or you went to the library and checked out a "how-to" book, or you bought one. We ordered a set of Time Life Home Improvement Books. These were lifesavers for us as a young married couple with big dreams. I can only imagine the mess we would have gotten into without those books.

It was the same with our second home. We bought an old farmhouse sitting on eight acres of land with a barn. I say farmhouse loosely. It was a shack. We bought it on the first walkthrough, shook hands on the deal under an old oak tree in the backyard with an elderly man who was too old to farm any more. It wasn't until he emptied the house of his fifty years' worth of belongings that we realized the whole thing needed to be gutted. I'm talking the interior walls, the exterior siding, and all of the electrical wiring. There was a back porch that we thought we would convert into our bedroom, but after all of his freezers were moved off the floor, we discovered it was a thin layer of concrete and was all busted up. It probably wasn't my most thought-out purchase. So, we packed up our three kids, moved into my parents' upstairs bedrooms. This time we needed an architect with real blueprints. We were slightly in over our heads. But two years later, with the help of lots of friends, we had a gorgeous home, twice the size of the original, and we did it without much professional assistance.

I can't imagine what the finished product would have been like without a plan. What started as an overwhelming undertaking, was made easier with a set of blueprints and a well-thought-out, step-by-step process. Sure, we had to improvise on occasion, but a plan helped the quality and ease of the project. By seeing the end goal—the finished product on paper and with a step-by-step process to carry us through each phase of the project, we created a finished home that gave us years of enjoyment.

Now, you're asking yourself, "What does this have to do with parenting? Am I reading a DIY book or a book on parenting?" the answer is *yes*. This is a book on parenting, but it is also a book on how to "do-it-yourself." It isn't simply a "quick-fix" guide. No. This is "That owners-manual you always thought should have come with your child." kind of book.

Think about all the DIY projects people have gotten into without a plan. Or, how frustrating it was for you that time you tried to put together some new toy you purchased without following the instruction guide. In so many of these, it was a "no harm, no foul" kind of a project. You mess up on putting a lawn mower together; you can start over. It's true with some things. Not so much with raising kids. Raising good kids is hard.

Contrary to conventional wisdom, you need a plan. The stakes are high. We're talking about lives here. So many people have to live with the consequences of your parenting. In reality, there aren't any do-overs in parenting. It's not like golf; you don't get a mulligan if you don't like the result.

It always amazes me to see young couples spend so much money on training their pet or on getting kids lessons in sports, cheering, dance, music, art, or martial arts. They will spend time figuring out how to get their four-year-old a college scholarship and yet have no plan to raise a kid that turns out to be an enjoyable adult, who you love to be around, who others love to be around, and who actually loves themselves.

Most of us have a real desire to be good parents. We care about our kids. We want nothing but the best for them. But life gets busy. We begin reacting to life as opposed to being proactive in our parenting. Then in a few years, we wonder how we got to this place where chaos is in full force. It seems our kids are constantly fighting, never content with the things they have. We quit going out to dinner because the chaos is not worth the effort. We lay our heads down at night and ask ourselves, "How did we get here?"

It's somewhere around this point I'll get an email or message from that parent saying, "Help!" Or, "Hey, can we get together and talk?" After listening to them tell me their troubles, and probing just a little, it becomes obvious. They chose this path.

It's always hard for a parent to believe that. They look at me and say, "You're crazy. I never wanted this! I always dreamed of having the perfect little family." We have a hard time as individuals, taking responsibility for our choices and actions. There is a failure to understand that our dreams and intentions, alone, don't take us to the place we desire. It is direction that does this.

Andy Stanley, a pastor, author, and leadership guru shares a principle in his book, *The Principle of the Path*, that says, "Direction, not Intention, determines our Destination."[1]

When we apply this to our parenting, we can see that our problem isn't that we're bad parents or that we aren't trying hard enough. The problem is we haven't focused enough on the end game, and as a result, we take steps away from the true direction that we want to take. We dream in one direction and then we "walk" in a different direction.

"Direction, not Intention determines our destination." Why is this so hard to see? I think, for one, we fall into what we call a "herd mentality." That's the adult version of peer-pressure. We fall into the trap of parenting the way our circle of friends parent. Or, we subconsciously imitate what we see in social media or on the shows we watch. It's the "everybody else is doing it, so maybe we should too" approach. Many parents are moving in the wrong direction, and we end up following them down that same path.

Secondly, it's easy to deceive ourselves about our own lives, choices, behaviors, and parenting skills. It's amazing how we can readily see in others what we can't see in ourselves. How many times have you come home from a night out with friends and thought, *No wonder their kids are crazy. Did you see the way he glared at them, the way she talked to them? Their kids were going crazy, and they didn't even try to calm them down.*

We all need someone that is a little further down the road than we are to coach us or to give us advice, maybe even serve as a consultant. We need objective input in our lives. We do that with our exercise training, our finances, and so much more. But when it comes to parenting, we think it should just come naturally. I hope this book will help you see the value in having someone journey with you in your season of parenting. Whether it is simply through this book, you attend one of our workshops or take one of our courses; I want to help you feel confident as you parent your children.

And finally, it's about our decision-making process. We tend to make decisions emotionally, what many call "impulse buying." We lean toward happiness. Our kids come up to us and say, "Please, please, please. Can't we get it? I wanna go there," and we give in. In truth, we do the same thing with many of the choices we make for our own lives. While happiness is enjoyable, sometimes the decision to be happy in the moment isn't the wisest thing to do for the long-haul. We have to ask ourselves as parents, "What is the best thing for the future hopes and dreams of our family?"

The answer for us, and I'm convinced for you as well, is in what Tammy and I call, the "Directional Parenting Blueprint." Children naturally flow through three phases of development. There is the *Discipline Phase* when we instill self-control in their lives. These are the zero to five-year-olds. What we do as we create the *Directional Parenting Blueprint* is envisioning what that child will look like going into first grade. What do we envision them knowing? What is their attitude like? What sort of self-image do they possess? How do they treat others? As we take the time now, while they are infants, and write down all of this, we begin to reverse-engineer a plan for how we will ensure that what we do moves us toward the blueprint. We do the same thing for the other two phases.

The *Training Phase* is where we focus on training them in how life works, relationally, emotionally, physically, and spiritually. So, we create a Directional Parenting Blueprint for this age, which are the six to twelve-year-olds, and we envision them on their first day of junior high school. We envision them relationally, emotionally, intellectually, and spiritually.

The third phase is the *Coaching Phase*. These are the thirteen to eighteen-year-olds. We focus on helping them see their strengths and weaknesses and how to use those to benefit themselves in life. So, we envision them during the summer of their high school graduation. And, like the other phases, we envision them in the same areas and then reverse engineer a process to lead our kids toward a healthy outcome so that we raise kids who we love to be around, and who others love to be around, and kids who love themselves—well-rounded kids relationally, emotionally, intellectually, spiritually, and physically.

This parenting journey you are on will require a change in you. Are you ready? Good parenting will always require more change in us than it will in our children.

CHAPTER TWO

YOU CANNOT NOT TEACH

Why how you were raised helps you become a great parent

My dad grew up in a time when, out of necessity, you had to know how to repair things yourself. On many of those occasions, I was the holder of the flashlight, especially while working on cars. At the time, it felt like the most boring job on the planet. It seemed that every time we worked on a car; it would be difficult. A bolt would break, or a part wouldn't fit. My dad would patiently work on it until he finally got the part on or off. And every time, I mean every time, he would say without fail, "Thank you, Lord!" As I grew up and began to work on my own cars, guess what I would say when the repair happened? Yep, I said, "Thank you, Lord!"

My mom has always been the inquisitive, prodding, loving friend. She had to check on everybody, and she seemed to know intuitively if someone was troubled, worried, or bothered. As I began pastoring, I found myself carrying on that same trait.

You see, there is this adage I learned a long time ago, "You cannot not teach." My mom, dad, and others who had an impact in my life taught me by example. Their impact wasn't in their lectures alone; it was by observing their attitudes, behaviors, and mannerisms.

It's important that before we press on and talk about the subject of raising kids who turn out right, we take a look in the rearview mirror and see how we were raised. We don't live life in isolation. You have children. You have history. We are a product of our parents or those who raised us., just as our parents are a product of our grandparents. We are bringing all of our baggage, good and bad, into this parenting thing. You and I are the result of our parents' influence: their mannerisms, their thought processes, their habits, and their sayings.

Some of you are thinking, *I'm nothing like my dad!* or *I'm nothing like my mom!* And you may be saying that to distance yourself from the fact that you believe your parents were terrible. Or, you may be saying it with the mindset that says, "I'll never be as good a parent as mine were."

Stored in our memory bank are all the experiences of our life. They seep out at times as we are living our lives. Sometimes we are even unaware. How many times do you find yourself saying things your parents told you, that you swore you would never say to your children? "Do you want a spanking?" (Yeah, Dad, that's exactly what I was thinking!) or "Do I look stupid to you?!" (Uh . . . is that a trick question?) Unless you make intentional choices to parent differently than your parents, old instinctive habits will surface.

So, before we take a look at how to raise kids who turn out right, we need to slow down and take an honest assessment of who we are. What we don't want to do is consciously bring unhealthy attitudes, values, and shortcomings into our children's lives.

Everything is parenting. Everything. Let that sink in. Parents influence and shape us whether they are grand-parents, step-parents, adoptive-parents, foster-parents, or any other type of parent. Since Adam and Eve, every-one has been raised by someone.

Parenting shapes much of our attitude, thought process, physical makeup, work ethic, worldview, and so much more. Your boss, your employees, your co-workers, all were shaped by their parents. In reality, everything you own, eat, or consume, is the result of parenting.

None of us arrive as adults without having been influenced by others. The influence may have been good or bad, but it's undeniable that others have had a profound effect on us. Remember, "You cannot not teach." What you will do as a parent, how you will par-ent, what you think, say, feel, and do, will shape your child's future.

Several years back, Tammy and I found ourselves at a difficult place in life. A series of internal conflicts within our ministry, a ministry we had launched and served for fifteen years, had led us to the place where we resigned. We were drained, hurt, and devastated. I've always been optimistic about life. I see the upside in everything. I'm never down. I'm either up, or getting up, but never down . . . except in this instant, I wasn't. On the suggestion and urging of a friend, we made our way out to Oklahoma City to a place called Renewal Ranch. It's an incredible, intimate place for hurting souls, led by our friends, Bob and Laura. It was here that I found one of the most helpful tools we've ever used to bring perspective and hope to our lives.

They had served us incredible meals, led us to a quiet pond on the ranch to sit and refresh. After a day of horseback riding, herding cattle, and an incredible steak dinner, we settled into the great room of their Ponderosa style home. It was an intimate setting, just Bob, Laura, Tammy, and me. They wheeled in a large whiteboard and began by asking me to draw a horizontal line through the middle of the board. Then, I was told to begin as early as I could remember and write down memorable moments. The ones that were positive, I was to write above the line and the negative ones below the line. It was done in chronological order. After that, it was Tammy's turn. And then, where our lives intersected, we both stood and filled out the graph.

What happened next was the most eye-opening experience we had ever had. Laura began to speak into our lives as she pointed out various memories to start to show us how they shape who we are. What we discovered in the process was the application of one of the Apostle Paul's statements to the Romans, "And we know that God causes everything to work together for the good of those who love God and are called according to his purpose for them."[2] It helped to propel us forward in life. It gave us clarity and perspective. It was like an emotional cleansing.

We began to use the "timeline" as it related to our marriage, our relationships, and our parenting, which is why I share this with you. Few things will help your parenting skills more than this mental, spiritual, and emotional exercise. Before you read another chapter, I encourage you to find a few hours, get a journal, or create something on your laptop to graph your own story. Then, grab your favorite beverage and reflect back over your life. This will give you a chance to see your failures and successes, your hurts and your hopes. You will see spots in your life that are potential landmines for your parenting. We have to bring our past out into the light, celebrate the good, and see the negatives in a fresh light so that we can be more effective in our parenting.

If you're a single parent, find a trusted friend and share this with them. If you have a mate at home, then they should be doing this as well. Once completed, sit down and share, compare, and contrast your lives, and give insight into each other. As you do this, you see your story unfold. You will see the highs and lows of your journey. Pray over this rearview timeline. As you do, you will see that what you thought was a deficit in your life was really an asset. You will see the ebb and flow of your life and how it can impact your kids' lives.

Because much of our parenting is a mental, emotional, and spiritual task, this will be one of the most important things you do as far as parenting is concerned.

CHAPTER THREE

NO CHILD IS A MISTAKE

*Seeing your child as a "gift" transforms
the way you parent*

I was sitting in my office one day as a young twenty-two-year-old student pastor. It was one of those days where I found myself alone at the church. The phone rang, and since I was the only one available, I picked it up. It's not something I ordinarily do, but I answered. It was one of our members who worked in the construction industry. He had called hoping to get our secretary to give him the number of Lifeline, our local adoption agency. It was before Google or cell phones. He said, "Can you find the number for me unless you know someone who wants to adopt a baby." He began to tell me how a father and daughter from a neighboring state had stopped at the construction site where he was working. The girl was pregnant, and they were looking to discreetly give the baby up for adoption if they could find someplace that would house them for a few months and pay for the delivery.

Tammy's sister and brother-in-law had wanted children early on in their marriage. After eight years of trying, they still found themselves childless and had begun talking about the possibility of adoption. So, when my friend told me the story, I said, "I actually do know someone who wants a baby. Let me call you back in a minute." I called Tammy, and she called her sister. Of course, her sister said yes, and after working out all the details, a few months later, our new little nephew was born. Now, some would say that was just random luck on our part, but we believe God heard the cries of our heart.

A few years later, believing it was not possible for them to have children, Tammy's sister found herself pregnant and they had another son. I believe there are no accidents when it comes to children being born. They are gifts from God, whether by adoption or birth. We had our middle son when Tammy was breastfeeding, and we were using contraception. Our youngest son was born thirteen years later, though we hadn't used birth control for about ten years.

It's important that you absorb this truth into your spirit. You have been given a gift. That child, those children that you have are a blessing. Let me say that again. Your kids are a blessing. Celebrate them. Sure, they may be a little messy. Sometimes they try your patience. Their strong will grates against you at times. Maybe they have issues that drive you crazy, but they are a treasure. Our tendency, as parents, is to see someone else's child and wish that ours was more like theirs. Don't do that. We have a saying that resonates in me as I work with parents, "Celebrate the kids you have, not the ones you wish you had."

It's also important for you to realize that your kids are blessed to have you as their parent. You, with all your insecurities about parenting, all the baggage that you bring into the relationship, are the one that God chose to give to your children to parent them, nurture them, guide them, and prepare them for life.

Dr. Luke, one of the traveling companions of the apostle Paul, wrote a journal during the beginnings of the early church. It's known as the Book of Acts, one of the books contained within the Bible. He makes a statement in that journal that is a powerful reminder concerning what we are talking about. He says, "From one man He made every nation of men, and He appointed the exact times and places where we should live."[3] Did you catch that? God appointed the exact time and place where you would be born. That means your children were appointed by God to be entrusted to you. Let that sink in. God desired you to have the kids you have right now! If He gave them to you, He can also equip you to care for them.

Before we begin an in-depth study of exactly how to raise our kids so they turn out right, I want to make sure we understand the miracle that your child's life is, as well as your own. Track with me here. It is a crazy but necessary thought. Your DNA is unique to you. There are approximately three billion letters that make up your DNA. You have about ten billion miles of DNA inside of you. Within that DNA you have about 20,000 genes that make you, you. Each one of your kids is different as well. Fabulously unique. Marvel at each one.

Now imagine with me that a round life preserver is floating in the Gulf of Mexico. Now let's say there is just one lone sea turtle swimming in all the oceans of the world, and she decides to pop her head out of the water to see what's going on. So, up she comes, and as her head breaks the surface of the water, she's right in the middle of that life preserver. Crazy odds, right? Well, those are the same odds that you, with your unique DNA makeup, your personality, would be born! That alone says that you are a miracle, and so is your child.

A woman begins life with approximately one million eggs. By the time she arrives at puberty, she has about 300,000. A man will generate over 500 billion sperm in his lifetime. The odds of your child, made up of their unique DNA, is 1 in 400 quadrillion. Add to that the number of people that you could have married, or birthed a child with, as well as your parents, and your mate's parents, all the grandparents and on down the line, and it becomes overwhelming to conceive of the sheer miracle that we are here.

I write all of this to help us change our mindset about how we see our kids. As you know, we have four kids spread out over eighteen years. As they are adults now, each one is a blessing, full of unique thoughts, ways, and ideas. I love being with each of them individually as well as collectively. I wish I had celebrated their uniqueness more than I did in their growing up years. I wish I had someone coaching me like I am hoping to do with you. We get one shot at this parenting thing. Enjoy every moment with those miracles we call our kids.

Tammy and I truly discovered the precious uniqueness as we began to see children through the perspective of being grandparents. We have grandkids scattered about the South. We have the Pardue's of Atlanta where two granddaughters live. Then there are the Patterson's of Oneonta, a little town about forty-five minutes out of Birmingham, where our daughter and her husband have given us three grandsons and a granddaughter.

Then we have the Pardue's of Nashville, where, at the moment, we have three grandsons. We have hopes that our youngest son, Jackson, will give us a few more.

As I write this chapter, we have just returned from a week with the Pardue's of Atlanta on the white sandy beaches of Destin. There is nothing like watching these two little girls interact. Harper Kate, the Princess of Peachtree, is my oldest granddaughter. As I mentioned earlier, she was born with about five different brain anomalies. While she can comprehend and process much of what happens, she can't walk, she can't talk, and she is fed through a feeding port in her stomach because she is unable to eat normally. There is no way to describe the impact this precious gift has had on me personally and to all who have come to hear her journey. She makes me a better person. She has a little devious personality that is so fun. Her big brown eyes dance when she gets excited. Her moans and grunts reveal a joy and love of life that few experience and her smile melts every heart that looks her way. She shares my love of the sun, sand, and noise of the gulf's waves. Her little sister, Allye Reese, The Queen of Everything, is a sassy teenager trapped in a preschooler's body. She is articulate, determined, and curious. Her exaggerated facial expressions make her theatrically appealing. Two very different girls in every way imaginable, but both precious in their uniqueness that is the miracle of life.

I don't know what your children are like, and I don't know whether you appreciate, celebrate, and cherish them, but I hope after reading this book, you will. Mindset is everything in parenting. Mindset is the windshield through which we see and determine how we will respond to our children. When we lose sight of their value, we react more harshly. When we fail to see parenting as a journey of developing our children into attractional adults, we don't enjoy the moments. Perspective and mindset are everything. So, let's celebrate our children and make sure they know it. Lavish them with it. Breathe in this season; it will pass quicker than you could ever imagine.

CHAPTER FOUR

A FRESH START BEGINS WITH HOPES AND DREAMS

Envisioning your child all grown up

I was deep in study one afternoon when my oldest son, Jarod, walked in from football practice. He was a junior in high school and strode into my office just off of our living room. He plopped down on the sofa near my desk and began talking about life. After a few minutes, he got up, said, "Well, I love you, Dad!" and bounced out of the room. It was at that moment that sheer panic welled up inside of me. It was at that moment I realized I only had eighteen months before he would be leaving for college. My mind raced with all of the things that I wanted to teach him and let him experience before he moved away to college.

I began to pray for wisdom and peace. Not long after I had finished praying, I was leaning back in my chair looking at my collection of books. My eyes landed on a youth ministry strategy binder that I used during my student ministry days. In those days, we used a ministry tool called a D.D.S. or Description of a Discipled Student. We would start with the end in mind. The thought process went like this; if a student came into my ministry as a seventh grader, what would I want them to look like when they graduated high school? What would we want them to know? What would we want them to think? What would we want them to feel? We spent hours writing that out. We were very specific in what the ideal student would look like. After we had written it out, analyzed it, prayed over it, and edited it, we began to work backward from there to design our student ministry. We designed our teaching to line up with our D.D.S. We designed our camps, retreats, activities, service projects, and mission trips to that end as well. We were reverse engineering our entire student ministry, keeping the end goal in mind.

It is done in so many areas of life. A business creates a purpose statement, values, and goals. Then they create policies and procedures. They create environments to accommodate the desired results. It's done in the construction industry as well. You begin by laying out all the desires, dreams, and goals of your dream house. An architect draws out the plans. They are very specific in every area, from plumbing to electrical, to the interior and exterior trim, as well as color. At that point, the building is reverse engineered to see to it that everything comes together just right.

So, with my mind flooded with our old student ministry days, I began to apply that to my oldest son.

It was the beginning of what we now call, "Directional Parenting Blueprint."

I made a list of all the things that I wanted him to know—truths and principles in the area of relationships, work ethic, core values, and biblical principles. Then there were practical issues like car repair, home repairs, and cooking. We listed experiences that he needed, like travel outside of the country—classic books that needed to be read. We wanted him to feel things, like a soft heart for the underprivileged, and to have a can-do mindset, as opposed to an "I can't" one. We wanted him to know how to have conversations with people of all economic classes, color, and age.

After we had listed everything out, we began to create a plan for the next eighteen months. Certain trips we would take, a list of books, and all the other things. We realized that with that blueprint in hand, we could relax and enjoy the next few months, not worrying about what we should do but just working our plan. It was life changing for us. When you know what you're trying to accomplish, and you've done the homework to map out the steps to make it happen, freedom is the result.

Most of you plan many areas of your lives. It could be your diet. You have a calorie plan or a low carb plan, or whatever diet is the fad of the moment. And you lay out everything that will happen so that your weight goal is hit in a reasonable time. You plan vacations, finances, and almost every other area of your life. Nothing is more important than planning what you want to see your children become as they move into adulthood.

So, here's how it works. I hope that your kids are young enough that you can plan for the long haul. But no matter your kids' age, it's essential to start now. Raising children breaks down easily into three different phases. There is what we call the *Discipline Phase*. That is the newborn to five-year-old. Then there is the *Training Phase*. This ranges from six years old to somewhere around twelve years old. Then there is the *Coaching Phase*. This is from thirteen years old to eighteen years old. Now, we never stop parenting. It's not like your job is done when they're eighteen, but everything changes around that time. We will look more closely and in greater detail at every phase of parenting in the next sections of the book. But for now, to get you thinking and dreaming, pick the phase that your child is in right now. If you have multiple kids, pick the phase for each one of them.

If you have a child in the *Discipline Phase*, I want you to imagine what they will look like as they head off to first grade. Begin asking questions. Jot down everything that comes to mind. You can categorize them later. Ask what kind of friend they will have? What kind of friend will they be? How will they treat their teacher? Will they know how to avoid a fight? Will they know how to carry on a conversation? Will they know how to deal with a stranger that approaches them? What things do you want them to know before they begin first grade? After you get all of this down, arrange it. Explore the best ways to instill those things into your child's life. Keep working until you are comfortable that the things you listed align with your purpose and goals.

If you have a child in the *Training Phase*, I want you to imagine what they will look like as they head off to junior high school. Scary, isn't it? It may be that you ask similar questions as before, but more exhaustive. You will most likely want to know how your son will treat a girl or how your girl will allow guys to treat them. As they move into sports, will they be a leader or follower? Will they know how to avoid a tempting situation? What study habits will they have? Will they be cliquish, or will they be able to move among the different subcultures and cliques of the school? What will they know spiritually? Will they know how to select healthy food and balance? What standards will they have in the area of movies, music, games, and apps?

If you have a child in the *Coaching Phase*, I want you to imagine what they will look like as they head off to college or begin their life beyond high school. Again, some of the questions will be similar to the other phases, but with a deeper layer. What kind of driver will they be? How will their bosses see them as they begin part-time work? Will they have an upbeat, positive view of life? Will they be fierce or fearful? Will they be able to change a flat tire or jump-start a car? Will they be loving? Gracious? Humble? Will there be confidence about them that draws others closer? How will they respond when the core values they hold are attacked as out of date or wrong and silly? Will they be able to bounce back from a broken heart? How will they handle betrayal? Will they have healthy financial habits?

As you begin to explore these areas, you are going to realize that what you're doing is shaping their values. Your kids will tend to inherit your values. What you may discover as you go through this process is that your values need shifting as well. So, as we have stated a few times already, you will most likely change as much as your kids will.

Now, we aren't going to worry about how we will ensure that our kids develop these values. This is just a first look. We will explore in great detail the "how" and the steps to take in the following sections. But I want to close this chapter with this philosophical truth. We all want our children to be people of character. Character is the result of behavior. How a person behaves on a daily basis reveals their true character. Behavior is always determined by attitude—how a person sees life. It's their world view, or their perspective. Attitude is the windshield through which they see life. Attitude is always shaped by thought. King Solomon, whom the Bible says was the wisest man who ever lived, said, "As a man thinks in his heart, so is he."[4] Literally, how we think affects everything else about us. It shapes us emotionally, physically, mentally, and spiritually. For change to take place, thinking has to change. What our kids think and believe affects their attitudes. Their attitudes will always affect how they behave in any given situation. Behavior lived out over time reveals their character and ultimately, their reputation.

Our hearts think, and our hearts desire. It's true of all of us. Wrong thoughts create wrong desires or attitudes, which always lead to wrong behavior. That's why teaching truth to your child is important. There is a short statement in the Bible that says that the Word of God, "judges the thoughts and attitudes of the heart." That's why time spent with your child understanding sound biblical principles is so important.

As parents, we are in the change business. It begins with feeding and filling our child's brain with truth, philosophies, and principles. So, get a journal, find a creative spot, and start laying out your "Directional Parenting Blueprint."

PART TWO

DEVELOPING A DIRECTIONAL BLUEPRINT

No one starts out building something or creating something without a plan, a blueprint, a clear vision of what the end product will look like.

CHAPTER FIVE

YOUR CHILD IS INCREDIBLY UNIQUE AND AWESOME

Discovering their internal make-up

It takes a bit of time as a parent to begin to see your baby awaken to their personality. Their uniqueness becomes much more apparent the more children you bring into the world. They may share some of your quirks, mannerisms, and humor; but as you observe them more closely, you notice that much of their behavior is nothing like yours. We begin wondering how these kids could be related to us. One of them is a compulsive neat freak, and the other thinks they're the life of the party, and you are neither of those things.

We assume our kids will react like we did when we were their age. As a result, we struggle and fight to get them to perform as we would in this journey we call life. If we're not careful, we make assumptions about our children concerning how they should react in certain situations.

If you have more than one child, you most likely have discovered that each one reacts to life in different ways. You see it in sleep patterns, how they respond to authority, what and how they eat, how they play with other kids, and how they put their toys away . . . or don't! No two kids are alike, but we all share one of four personality types.

Tammy and I first began learning about personality types when we were a newly married couple. I've always been off the chart optimistic, and she is more on the cautious, steady side. I'm a risk taker, but her . . . not so much. Early in our marriage, I began to get a little frustrated at what I thought was this negative, disapproving attitude she had about all my great ideas and dreams. We were in Arrowhead Springs, California, being trained in student ministry, and the class was about the four personality types. They were using the DISC Personality Profile Assessment tool. It was there that I had an "aha!" moment. I realized that Tammy wasn't negative or pouring cold water on all my dreams; she was functioning in her God-given personality as a critical thinker. I saw her as a partner who could help my dreams become more successful as she saw potential landmines along the way. We became trained in the use of the DISC Profile and began to assess our children who were toddlers at the time. It was such fun when we began to discover the uniqueness of each one.

Each of your children has a uniqueness about them as well. The Creator wired each of us with a personality. He created a great diversity in us. King David of Israel, said, "For you created my inmost being; you knit me together in my mother's womb."[5] Isn't that incredible to think about? When you were pregnant with your baby, imagine God weaving together that little miracle. Not just the body, but the inner person as well. God entrusted you with the gift of the children you have. They are, in a sense, your assignment from the Creator. King Solomon, the son of King David and his wife, Bathsheba, wrote, "Children are a gift from the Lord; they are a reward from Him."[6] Amazing isn't it? And these little gifts come pre-wired in a unique fashion. Each one is different. Some are more confident, and others are a little more insecure. Some will have a weak disposition, and some will be strong. You may have one that is an out-of-the-box leader, or they may respond more as a follower. One may be more stubborn and challenging to the status quo while still another will be more compliant and eager to please. Some will be light-hearted, and one may be so serious, they have a meltdown if life isn't just as they think it should be. Now, while some of this is the result of their social environment, much of it is the result of the makeup of their personality.

Our goal isn't to make them just like us, to turn them into our "mini-me." We want to take who they are and shape and guide them according to the way God created them. We don't want to change them into something they weren't designed to be, but to help them soar. We teach them how to rein in some of the extremes in their personality and how to bolster up some of the weaknesses they may be prone to.

No one personality is better than the other, or more right, or more wrong. They're all different. Different isn't wrong; it's merely different. It is these different personalities that will make your family unique and fun. It is important to understand the danger in seeking to shape our kids into our mold or personality type. To do so is to invite rebellion in their heart as they grow up. Aesop, who wrote so many cherished fables that kids have been reading for years, said about children, "The bow that is always bent will soon break." His point was that we can't always be pressuring kids to perform in a certain way, or we will break them. While it is our job to shape how they think, guiding the attitude that flows from that thinking, we want to give them room to let it flow out in a way that is comfortable to them.

It is an essential principle to grasp if we are to be effective parents. Solomon said a similar thing in a proverb, often quoted among parents, that says, "Train up a child in the way that he should go, and when he is old he will not depart from it."[7] While most use this passage as assurance that their wayward child will return to the right and moral path, that is not the sole point. The Hebrew word in that proverb for "the way he should go," is better translated, "in the way he is bent." The application of this truth is that we have a responsibility as parents to train our children in the morality of thought, attitude, and behavior within the way they are "bent," or according to their unique design.

As we began teaching personality traits and how to "get along" with each other, it all came together for our parenting skills when we read a little book called, *The Treasure Tree*, by John Trent and Gary Smalley.[8] In the book, the four personality types are demonstrated by the animal kingdom; the Lion, the Otter, the Beaver, and the Golden Retriever. It was another "aha!" moment for us.

Since then, we have used those animals in our parenting workshops, marriage seminars, and business team-building sessions we offer.

Hippocrates, an ancient Greek physician, introduced the world to the four types. Today it is understood that all of us are born with a bent toward a certain personality.

These rarely change over time. It's almost as though we have these traits locked in our DNA from birth. These are best seen by placing them on a quadrant.

Each of your kids will tend to be more extroverted or introverted. Extroverts tend to be a little quicker in decision making or instigating change. Introverts tend to take a little more time making decisions and are slow to embrace change. Within each of those traits, your child will tend to be more "people" oriented or "task" oriented. If we were to put it on a quadrant, it would look like this:

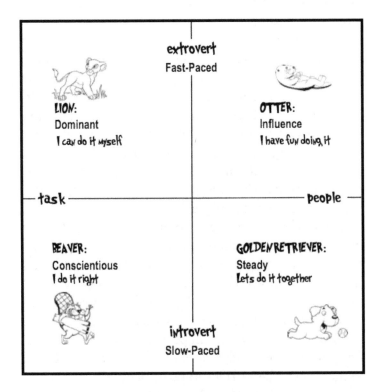

In the upper half of the quadrant are the extroverts and in the bottom half are the introverts. The farther they are away from the center line, the more extreme they will function in that area. The extrovert, depending on how far up from the line they are, will be more fast-paced in decision-making. It is similar for the introverts. The further below the line they are, the slower-paced and more cautious they are in making decisions. Extroverts process information a lot faster, while the introvert tends to sift through information a little slower. Change will come quicker for the extrovert, while the introvert needs a little more time to process the change. It is not an intellectual thing; it is a personality thing. You and your kids will fall into one of those two categories.

Now, when we look at the quadrant from left to right, we place those people who tend to be more task-oriented on the left side of the grid and those who tend to be more relational oriented on the right side. The task-oriented people are anxious to get things done. The extrovert will have their way of doing that. They will take charge and "conquer the task." The introvert will be more methodical, out-thinking everyone else. They will take their time, making sure all the necessary steps and pieces are in place. Now, to be placed into the task side of the grid doesn't mean you don't get along with people or that there is something socially wrong with you. It merely means that you see life as a series of tasks. On the right side, we place those who are more about people relationally. For the extrovert, it will mean that they see everyone as their buddy. They are the life of the party and make everyone feel included. The introvert will have deeper relationships and will be more loyal, best-friend type of people.

We take our clients and workshop attendees through a test so they can personalize and define exactly where everyone is on the graph. It's always a highlight of the workshops when everyone can laugh at themselves and find encouragement at the same time.

It is critical in our parenting journey that we understand the strengths and weaknesses of each of our children based on their personalities. Each one will bring a different viewpoint into the family dynamic. Each will see life through the perspective of their "animal." Knowing this helps you see situations that come up from their perspective. It will change how you respond and connect with each child. It will also help each child move within the family with comfort and confidence. In the next few chapters, we will do a deep-dive into each of the four personality types.

CHAPTER SIX

RAISING A LION, I CAN DO IT MYSELF

Shaping the dominant child

If you have a *lion* in your family, then you can usually spot them right away. They are King of the Jungle. The lion is an extrovert who leans toward the task or doer-oriented side of the quadrant. They are the "D" in the DISC profile, which stands for Dominant. These are also known as "Choleric." Their mantra is, "I can do it myself."

The younger the child, the less obvious some of these traits will be. But the quick snapshot of them is that they want to see results from their efforts. If you have older children, you will notice that they are what we call "bottom line" people. In conversations, they like for others to get to the point. If they think something needs to be done, they take action. They solve problems. They don't like the status quo. They always think there is a better way. If you give them a chance, they will figure out a way to do it better, quicker, and engage others to make it happen.

They don't like the word *no*. They are like little bulldogs. They have a stubborn streak in them, and they will figure out a way to get what they want. They aren't intimidated by authority because they think they should be in control. They like to make the rules.

You should expect your lion to be very competitive. They truly hate to lose at anything. They turn creative to find any way to win because losing is simply not an option. Your little lion is determined and strong-willed. I know you're thinking, *Every kid I have is strong-willed!* While it is true that we all tend toward a self-absorption that plays itself out in fighting for what we want, the lion is at another level altogether. They will challenge you, your authority, and your wisdom. All of this will make them impatient and demanding, determined, and outspoken.

The lion is curious; they love to discover new things and to break things apart to see how they work. They love an adventure.

They are natural leaders. There is a confidence about them, even if they are wrong. They tend toward independence and are generally self-sufficient. They rarely get emotional. To them, it is a sign of weakness. Don't expect them to cry at movies or when some sad event happens. They will use anger as their outlet.

As a leader, they are goal oriented. They will figure out how to get others to do their work. If we ever asked Jarod to do a task like taking out the garbage or picking up the toys, he would instinctively turn around to his brother or sister and say, "We need to take the trash out," or "We need to pick up the toys."

Their strengths, when not channeled in a healthy direction, will mean that they can tend toward being bossy, impatient, quick-tempered, argumentative, inflexible, unsympathetic, and rarely give compliments. They can be manipulative and speak out in a rash or harsh manner.

As friendships go, they see little need for friends. But if you are their friend, expect them to be honest with you about their opinions. When an emergency arises, or you are in trouble, they step right in and take charge. The downside is that they tend to use people. They can be domineering and have a know-it-all mentality. They don't mind deciding for others. They will always think they can do everything better than you. They have a hard time apologizing. The upside is that they are usually unaffected by peer-pressure, but they are good at pressuring others.

LION overall cheat-sheet:
adventurous, determined, outspoken, competitive, strong-willed, busy, focused, hard worker, impatient, demanding

Emotional strengths:
a born leader, dynamic and active, feels the need to correct wrongs, strong-willed and decisive, unemotional, appears confident, independent and self-sufficient

Emotional weaknesses:
bossy, impatient, quick-tempered, can't relax, argues, won't give up when losing, inflexible, not complimentary, dislikes emotion, unsympathetic

Family strengths:
leads with authority, goal oriented, delegates tasks to others, motivates to action, fast thinker, knows the right answer, organizes, sees the big picture, thrives on opposition

Family weaknesses:
intolerant of mistakes, makes rash decisions, can be seen as rude or mean, manipulative, demanding, demands loyalty, answers too quickly, hates poor performance

Friend strengths:
has little need for friends, is usually right, good in emergencies

Friend weaknesses:
tends to use people, domineering, know-it-all, decides for others, can do everything better, can't apologize

This child walks into a room and takes charge. They make quick decisions as to what to play with, who to play with, and how everyone will play. They most likely will be the teacher's pet because they are good with responsibility. They are relatively independent and not easily influenced.

Take a few moments and look back over this chapter. Not everything laid out will be true of your lion. You will want to make a list of strengths and weaknesses of your lion and develop well-thought-out responses and actions to lead them to understand themselves and how to soar in their strengths and be cautious concerning their weaknesses.

CHAPTER SEVEN

RAISING AN OTTER, I WANNA HAVE FUN

Steering the playful child

If you have an *otter* in your family, they'll keep you laughing. They are the playful creature of the sea. The otter is an extrovert who leans toward the people or relational side of the quadrant. They are the "I" in the DISC profile, which stands for "Influence." They are also known as "Sanguine." Their mantra is, "I have fun doing it."

As with the lion, the younger the child, the less obvious some of these traits will be. But the quick snapshot of them is that they want to have fun. They have a great desire to enjoy life, and they don't take it so seriously. They make friends easily because of their optimistic, easy going, playful personality. They love to talk. Did I say they love to talk? As an older teen, they will be the one who is at a party telling tales. Their imagination will cause them to exaggerate events if it makes others laugh.

They have a short attention span, and they are constantly looking for the next play toy or party. They don't like rules. If there are rules, they will always try to change them. They love to take a dare—to risk what they have just for a little fun. They are natural leaders who everyone follows without a fight. They love to be the center of attention.

You should expect your otter to be a little messy and seemingly disorganized. Remember that they see life not through tasks, but through relationships. They live life for the moment, for the adventure. As a result, they leave toys on the floor when the next great adventure comes into their mind. They will do anything for a laugh and see the humor in life. They will keep your family laughing. They have a kind and sincere heart. Your otter will be emotional. They will cry and laugh and engage in life with everything they have. They can appear egotistical, talking about themselves in their stories, and they can seem phony and a little too happy for some.

Relationally, they make good first impressions. Anytime you are with an otter one-on-one, they will make you feel like you are one of their closest friends. The reality is, they have many "friends." They see everyone as their friend but can't always remember names that well. So, everyone is Buddy, Girl, or another generic nickname like Sunshine or Stud. They influence others. Some of it is subtle manipulation. They are great motivators and can get others to do things they wouldn't ordinarily do. The otter has a certain charm or attraction about them. Their enthusiasm and energy is attractive. The downside is that they can keep the home in a frenzy and a little disorganized. They don't always tell the whole story. They need to be approved by others, so telling the truth about wrongs comes hard for them.

The upside of the otter is that they are fun-loving, encouraging, forgiving, and extremely motivating. The downside is that they tend to be undisciplined, make emotional decisions, and are forgetful.

OTTER overall cheat-sheet:
playful, sociable, talkative, lively, imaginative, people-person, messy, cheerful

Emotional strengths:
likable personality, storyteller, talkative, life of the party, good sense of humor, emotional and demonstrative, enthusiastic, curious, lives in the present, sincere at heart

Emotional weaknesses:
compulsive talker, exaggerates, can't remember names, too happy for some, egotistical, naive-gets suckered, controlled by the environment, seems phony

Family strengths:
makes home fun, liked by other kids' parents, volunteers for duties, thinks up new activities, looks good on the surface, creative, energetic enthusiasm, motivates others to join, charming

Family weaknesses:
keeps home frenzied, disorganized, doesn't listen to the whole story, doesn't follow through, undisciplined, makes emotional decisions, easily distracted

Friend strengths:
makes friends easily, loving, thrives on compliments, envied by others, doesn't hold grudges, quick to apologize, spontaneous

Friend weaknesses:
dislikes being alone, needs attention, looks for credit, dominates conversations, interrupts and doesn't listen, answers for others, forgetful, bends the truth

This child makes a grand entrance and brings life into a room. They love to tell stories and be the center of attention. They love life and want others to as well. They usually talk too much but are loved by most and are easily distracted.

Take a few moments and look back over this chapter. Not everything laid out will be true of your otter. You will want to make a list of strengths and weaknesses of your otter and develop well-thought-out responses and actions to lead them to understand themselves and how to soar in their strengths and be cautious in their weaknesses.

CHAPTER EIGHT

RAISING A BEAVER, I DO THINGS RIGHT

Seeing the careful child

If you have a *beaver* in your family, they'll make sure you keep all the rules. They are the industrious creatures of the freshwater. The beaver is an introvert who leans toward the task or doer side of the quadrant. They are the "C" in the DISC profile, which stands for "Conscientious." They are also known as "Melancholy." Their mantra is, "I do things right."

The quick snapshot of the beaver is that they are cautious and thorough. They are keenly aware of what's right and what's wrong. They are specific when it comes to facts of a situation. The beaver doesn't quit; they love to see projects through to the end.

They're not much on getting dirty or messy. They usually have a place for everything. They love to take things apart and put them back together. They are the "questioneers." They love to ask why or what-if. They love the routines and traditions of life. They are rule-keepers and worry about what might happen if we break the rules. They expect the worst and plan for every disaster. They have a long attention span and love mental challenges.

You should expect your beaver to be somewhat of a perfectionist. They see life as a series of tasks to be performed. They are detailed and orderly. When they are packing for a trip, they won't forget critical items. They are critical thinkers and want to know how things work. Your beaver will, for the most part, keep their stuff neat and orderly.

From an emotional standpoint, the beaver is a deep thinker. They are analytical, philosophical, conscientious, and serious. They stay on task. The downside is that they are critical and remember the negatives. They love to be alone. They are too introspective, which leads to unhealthy guilty feelings.

Your beaver makes friends cautiously and is somewhat content to stay in the background. They are a devoted friend who listens well, has a deep concern for others, and is compassionate. They are great at solving problems for you. Their weakness is that they live through others and are socially insecure. They can be withdrawn, holding back affection. They dislike opposition and can become suspicious and unforgiving.

BEAVER overall cheat-sheet:
detailed, orderly, persistent, respectful, deep, neat, careful, hard to please, rule-keeper

Emotional strengths:
deep, analytical, serious and purposeful, smart, artistic, philosophical, sensitive to others, self-sacrificing, conscientious

Emotional weaknesses:
remembers the negatives, moody, depressed, false humility, off in their own world, low self-image, selective hearing, self-centered, too introspective, harbors guilt feelings

Family strengths:
sets high standards, wants everything done right, keeps the home in order, picks up after others, sacrifices own will for others, encourages study and talent, schedule oriented, perfectionist, detail-minded, persistent and thorough, organized, economical, sees problems and finds solutions, needs to finish what they start, likes graphs, charts, and lists.

Family weaknesses:
goals are beyond reach, can tend to discourage, too much about details, becomes the martyr, pouts, not people oriented, hesitant to start projects, spends too much time planning, hard to please, needs too much approval

Friend strengths:
makes friends cautiously, content to stay in the background, avoids attention, devoted, listens, problem-solver, deep concern, compassionate

Friend weaknesses:
lives through others, socially insecure, withdrawn, too critical of others, holds back affections, dislikes opposition, suspicious, unforgiving

This child doesn't like parties. They love order and worry too much about stuff. They keep the rules and hold others to them as well. They find one friend and stay with them.

Take a few moments and look back over this chapter. Not everything laid out will be true of your beaver. You will want to make a list of strengths and weaknesses of your beaver and develop well-thought-out responses to lead them to understand themselves and how to soar in their strengths and be cautious in their weaknesses.

CHAPTER NINE
RAISING A GOLDEN RETRIEVER, LET'S DO IT TOGETHER

Steadying the steady child

If you have a *Golden Retriever* in your family, you will have found your cuddle-buddy. Of all the animals in the kingdom, they are "man's best friend." The retriever is an introvert that leans toward the people or relational side of the quadrant. They are the "S" in the DISC profile, which stands for "Steady." They are also known as "Phlegmatic." Their mantra is, "Let's do it together."

The quick snapshot of them is that they are easygoing. There is a peacefulness about them that draws you in. They are thoughtful, patient, and loyal. They usually go to bed without a fight. They don't mind sharing their toys and books. They tend to be a follower of others. They are people-pleasers and are loyal to their close friends. They are a little slower when eating, brushing their teeth, and getting ready for bed.

From an emotional standpoint, they have a low-key personality, are easygoing and relaxed. They tend to have a well-balanced, consistent life. While they are somewhat quiet, they are sympathetic and kind. They can take the good with the bad and are slow to get upset. They tend toward an emotional weakness of being unenthusiastic, fearful, and worried. They can be indecisive and avoid responsibility. They don't like change and need time to prepare for it. It is possible for them to be too compromising.

As a friend, they are easy going, pleasant, enjoyable, inoffensive, and a good listener. They love deep, long-term friendships. The downside is that they can dampen enthusiasm and seem indifferent or judgmental.

GOLDEN RETRIEVER overall Cheat-sheet:
thoughtful, controlled, adaptable, attentive, diplomatic, loyal, patient, easygoing, helpful

Emotional strengths:
low-key personality, easygoing and relaxed, patient, well-balanced, consistent life, quiet but witty, sympathetic and kind, hides emotions

Emotional weaknesses:
unenthusiastic, fearful and worried, indecisive, avoids responsibility, selfish, shy, too compromising, self-righteous

Family strengths:
takes time for family, is not rushed, takes the good with the bad, slow to get upset, competent at work, peaceful

and agreeable, administrative, mediator, avoids conflict, finds the easy way

Family weaknesses:
slack on discipline, disorganized, not goal oriented, lacks motivation, slow to change, lazy and careless, too passive and non-participatory

Friend strengths:
easy going, pleasant, enjoyable, inoffensive, good listener, dry humor, people watcher, lots of deep friendships, compassionate and concerned

Friends weaknesses:
dampens enthusiasm, stays uninvolved, not exciting, indifferent, judgmental, resists change

They enter the room slowly and find enjoyment in watching others have fun. They are fond of noise and usually give in to whatever the other person wants. They have a deep love for others.

Take a few moments and look back over this chapter. Not everything laid out will be true of your Golden Retriever. You will want to make a list of strengths and weaknesses for them and develop well-thought-out responses and actions to lead them to understand themselves and how to soar in their strengths and be cautious in their weaknesses.

PART THREE
WALKING TODDLERS THROUGH THE DISCIPLINE PHASE

Helping a child learn self-control can be exhausting. The better we can aid them in developing this, the easier the other phases of life will become. Here, you will find tips and strategies to successfully meet the challenges of this phase.

CHAPTER TEN
GETTING THEM UNDER CONTROL
How to build "self-control" not "selfishness" in your child

In my younger days, I spent a few weeks every summer at a little camp in South Alabama. There was a gentle old soul there named Samson that tended to the horses. He had a slow Southern drawl and had a love for the children who gathered each week of the summer. Among my duties as camp speaker, and cabin leader, I would help him with the horses. We would feed, brush, bridle, and saddle the horses and then unbridle, unsaddle, and brush the horses down before letting them loose to roam at the end of the day. During one of those weeks, he taught me about breaking horses. He said, "You always want to be careful to break the horse's *will* and not their *spirit*." He then began to tell me that the best time to break a horse is when they are a foal, a baby horse, not when they are older. He went on to tell me that if you tie the horse for a few minutes several times a day on a short rein when they are older, and you want to saddle them, they are easy to train. He said the same thing applies to children.

I never forgot that lesson. If you help create order when your babies are young, it is less difficult to train them as they get older. You can never start too early. When you're trying to change that baby's diaper, and they start kicking, if you squeeze those little thighs gently and hold them still, while saying "no," and you do it consistently, they will stop fighting you.

A baby, brand new to this thing called life, is a bundle of selfishness. I know you probably think I shouldn't say that out loud, but it's true. Babies are sly little creatures. They get you all focused on how cute they are and how much they look like you. All of this is designed to give cover to their selfishness. They rarely wait for a convenient time to want to be fed. When they want to eat, they will cry and cry until you give in. They will dirty that diaper at the worst time. And then they will cry until you change them. But while you are changing them, they will wiggle and kick and see if you have what it takes to put a diaper on an octopus. They also have this game they play when you want to put them to bed. You'll lay them down and pat their little backside in a rhythmic sort of way until you think they are asleep. You will slowly raise one finger off of them at a time until your hand is no longer touching them. Then, you will gently walk, or sometimes crawl, out of the room, hoping for a little peace and quiet. Usually, just as you get to the door, they will crank up the crying as if to say, "No sleep for you yet!"

Built into every one of us is the "dirty-rotten-stinkin '-little-sinner" syndrome. We are all born with a self-preservation mindset. Have you noticed that you never have to teach a child how to lie? No one ever sits down with their child and says, "Today I want to teach you how to get out of trouble by lying." Lying is instinctive in all of us. Kids lose their temper and get mad when things don't go their way. They will pout, stomp, cry, hit, or scream, when things happen in their world that they don't like. Children will take things they want, not caring who those things belong to. Welcome to parenthood.

The early years of our children's lives establish much of how they see themselves, how they see others, and how they see the world. It is easy to get distracted, watching them explore the newness of living. If we're not careful, we will get caught up in the routine of life and not see ourselves as what we truly are. We are field guides to these little masterpieces of God's creation. It is our privilege and responsibility to help them see the wonder of the world, to lavish them with love, grace, and mercy, and to warn and train them to recognize the hidden dangers.

Our goal as a parent during this newborn to toddler phase is to instill self-control in them. It is a quality that is essential for their survival. This one trait is what unlocks their ability to thrive in life as they get older. From this one discipline, the discipline to keep ourselves under control flows the power to love ourselves, and others. Out of it flows compassion, integrity, a healthy work ethic, and the desire to care physically for the body that houses who we are. It tempers emotions while allowing them to flow in a healthy manner.

Self-control is what will make our children a joy to others. It is the subtle quality that will draw others to want to be friends with them. A self-controlled child has a grateful heart, giving respect and concern for others. Self-control keeps them from self-destructive behaviors while building healthy self-esteem.

For this to happen, they need discipline. When we hear the word discipline, most of us think of some punishment. Depending on how you were raised, many of you will think this means spanking, timeouts, or withholding something of perceived value from the child. The usual pattern is played out in one of several ways. "Son, stop trying to take that toy from your sister!" He does it again, and so we say, "Did you hear me?" Well, of course, they did. The problem isn't that they're deaf; it's that they are selfish. So, you pull a saying from your playbook of parenting options. A) "Don't make me count to three!" B) "If you don't stop, I'm putting you in timeout!" C) "If you don't stop, you're not getting any dessert tonight!" or D) "Go to my room, you're getting a spanking!" While these may temporarily stop him from hitting his sister, we have only modified his behavior . . . for the moment.

Discipline does not always equal punishment. The word discipline comes from the Greek word "disciple," meaning one who learns. In school, learning is encouraged by helping a student learn truths, facts, and ways in an organized manner. In reality, discipline is about creating self-control to bring about order. It is essential that we understand the goal of discipline isn't punishment; it is to create self-control.

In society, we have rules and laws to aid us in maintaining self-control. The penalty for driving under the influence is meant to help you choose not to get behind the wheel of a car if you have had too much to drink. Mature people do not need these rules or laws. They understand that the consequences of the rule go beyond punishment; it is meant to save others and themselves from danger. The rule becomes unnecessary when self-control and order have been learned and exercised. The same holds true of parenting. We give rules or principles to help our children develop self-control. Our goal is to create order, a life not lived by chaos but by principles.

While the goal of discipline early-on begins with modifying their behavior, it is not simply their actions that we should focus on. That's where too many parents go wrong. Our goal is to reach their hearts. Hearts are always shaped by what our mind thinks about the things that come into our lives. Our goal isn't to modify behavior alone, but to transform their thoughts away from focusing on themselves and toward a greater focus on others. It is the essence of the goal when our children are in this Discipline Phase. We must help them see why self-control is essential.

Most parents are reactionary when it comes to disciplining their child. The child does something that irritates us, and we lash out at them. It sometimes happens when our kids embarrass us or make us look bad. When we discipline from a reactionary position, we tend to do so from an unhealthy mindset. Not only that, but it sends confusing signals to our children. Because reactionary parenting is conditioned on our emotions, it tends to be inconsistent. It is important that we become proactive in our parenting to be directional. Remember, we all intend to raise good kids. We all intend to be good parents. But direction, not intention, gets us to our destination. It is so important to keep the end goal in mind. For the zero to five-year-old, the end game is self-control. Our goal is to lead them to a healthy place mentally, emotionally, physically, and spiritually. So, the question is, how do we do that?

CHAPTER ELEVEN

TO SPANK OR NOT TO SPANK

A look at what the Bible has to say

I grew up in the South when it was a normal activity in our childhood to get a spanking. You've most likely heard your parents or grandparents speak of having to go out and cut their own switch from the backyard. Or, they might tell you of the fierce sound of a belt being pulled through the pant loops at such speed that it sounded like a machine gun going off. Parent's in those days reached for whatever was handy to give a "whoopin'" when needed. In reality, I can think of only a handful of spankings I was given growing up.

As Tammy and I were raising our first three kids, few were questioning spanking as a natural, expected form of discipline. Today, it is a topic that divides our culture. I believe you can raise well-balanced children without spanking, and I think you can turn out well-balanced children with spanking. My goal here isn't to convince you of the rightness or wrongness of spanking, but to assist you in understanding the goal and guiding principles in this area as you strive to raise kids who turn out right.

Spanking is not merely punishing a child for a wrong, and certainly, no one should spank out of anger. We are about directional parenting, and to do that in a loving, controlled, intentional way. The purpose would be for correction. Most spankings are not even necessary. And in many cases, they happen spontaneously and more out of anger than correcting.

It is essential that parents know the difference between childishness and rebellion. Spilling milk is a child being a child. Throwing the bottle across the room is an act of defiance. A child running around and knocking something over is childishness. A child running, after you told them to stop, is rebellion. We should never punish a child for a childish act. They should always be dealt with for a rebellious act.

The Bible reveals a principle, not a command. The principle is this; correcting your children while there is hope. It should be in their early years that this happens, while there is hope. What we do in these first years pays big dividends later on.

Here are the relevant passages in the Bible. They are found in the writings of King Solomon, who wrote a series of proverbs to share the wisdom he had learned throughout his life. It was said of Solomon that God made him the wisest person to have walked the earth. We would do well, whether a Christian or not, to explore the Book of Proverbs. It is important to remember that these are not promises, but rather principles.

Whoever spares the rod hates their children,
    but the one who loves their children is careful
    to discipline them.
                                    —Proverbs 13:24

Diligence is the key issue in this principle. There is to be a consistency to our discipline. To become lazy in discipline is to be unloving. This is why it is important to lay out the blueprint of what qualities, attitudes, and values you want to see in your child. Once these are laid out, you can determine the best way to go about instilling them in your children.

Discipline your son while there is hope;
    do not set your heart on his destruction.
                                    —Proverbs 19:18[9]

It is a reminder that bad habits are hard to break. The older a child gets, the harder it is to break unhealthy attitudes and actions. Solomon paints the issue in stark contrasts. In his mind, to not diligently discipline a young child is to desire failure in the child as he moves into adulthood.

Folly is bound up in the heart of a child,
    but the rod of discipline drives it far from him.
                                    —Proverbs 22:15[10]

Again, we are reminded that all of us start out leaning toward selfishness, self-absorption, and chasing after foolishness. It is human nature to stay away from what brings us pain. If you've ever been stung by a wasp or hornet, then you know firsthand how your body jumps at the sound of one of them buzzing by your ear. We learn quickly to avoid that area, and no one needs to remind us of the danger. Spanking has the same effect on a small child.

> Do not withhold discipline from a child;
>> if you punish them with the rod, they will not die.
> Punish them with the rod and save them from death.
>> —Proverbs 23:13-14

Children need to be punished in a way that teaches self-discipline. The poetry of this phrase is one of contrast. He is not implying that we beat a child to near death. His point is that spanking a child does not bring death, but life. The failure to discipline a child is what puts him on a destructive path which leads to death.

> The rod and reproof give wisdom,
>> but a child left to himself brings shame to his mother.
>> —Proverbs 29:15[11]

Wisdom comes to us most often after we have failed. Children need help in gaining wisdom about choices and attitudes. A spanking and a conversation can help drive wisdom deep into them. When this is not done, that child will not develop self-control and will become self-absorbed and create a sense of embarrassment, shame, and grief on the parent.

> Discipline your son, and he will give you rest;
>> he will give delight to your heart.
>> —Proverbs 29:17[12]

There is nothing like an unruly child to disrupt the peace. Most of us know what it's like when we go out to dinner as a family, only to have the entire gathering of diners twisting their necks around, bulging their eyeballs in our direction because our precious child is throwing food and whining about every little thing at a volume that rivals a fire engine. I get that there are lots of reasons that could contribute to the scene, but most of the time, it is due to a lack of training and discipline. When we have diligently disciplined our children so that they behave, it brings a rest like nothing else.

Now, this next passage of Scripture is about the discipline the Lord gives to those who are His. Reading it provides us a sense of understanding—the "why" behind the "pain" associated with discipline.

> My son, do not regard lightly the discipline of the Lord, nor lose courage when you are punished by him. For the Lord disciplines him whom he loves, and chastises every son whom he receives.
>
> It is for discipline that you have to endure. God is treating you as sons; for what son is there whom his father does not discipline? If you are left without discipline, in which all have participated, then you are illegitimate children and not sons. Besides this, we have had earthly fathers to discipline us and we respected them. Shall we not much more be subject to the Father of spirits and live? For they disciplined us for a short time at their pleasure, but he disciplines us for our good, that we may share his holiness. For the moment, all discipline seems painful rather than pleasant; later, it yields the peaceful fruit of righteousness to those who have been trained by it.
>
> —Hebrews 12:5-11

This passage is rich with encouragement. It is a reminder that God's greatest desire for us is to walk and behave in a manner that is right, moral, and selfless; and so, like a good parent, disciplines us as well. Go back and read that passage again. Our goal is to discipline our children not in a careless, inconsistent way that brings frustration, but in a way that leads to the peace that comes with them doing the right things.

In his toddler years, one of my sons had a strong will. He was (and is) very determined, in a good way. But there was a time when he started touching the controls on our stereo sound system. I told him to stop. He looked at me. Keeping his eyes locked with mine, he touched it again! I got down on his level, looked him in the eye, and in a stern voice, said, "Don't touch that." As he reached for it again, I popped his little hand and said, "No!" He looked at me, sat down, and cried. In a matter of seconds, he reached for the system again. At that point, I knew I was in a battle of wills. Now, not every battle is a battle of the will. We have to learn as parents to pick our battles. But this was that battle. I may be exaggerating a little here, but I think I popped that little hand about twenty-eight times before he gave up.

That day was a defining moment for us. It was as if a light was turned on in him. He had an "aha!" moment. The goal is to break the will, not the spirit. Our goal isn't to alter their personality or take away their fun and curiosity, but to lead them in such a way that they learn how to control those impulses and desires. Modifying their behavior is basic at this age, as we train them to think differently. Remember, the ultimate goal is to teach how they think, which will affect their attitude, which will drive and direct their behavior.

As parents, we get to choose the method that we will use to bring about self-control. Some will spank, some will use a timeout. What you can't do is nothing.

Spanking early in the child's life is the quickest and surest way to instill self-control. It is also the one that will allow you to be the most consistent with disciplining them. This only works when you have clear rules, parameters, and principles that you have cemented in your own mind. Again, to discipline from emotion, whether in anger, stress, or embarrassment, is destructive to your child.

The benefit of spanking is that when it's done, it's over. They did wrong, a "pop" was given with a reason carefully explained, the child is loved, and life goes on.

A timeout is harder to maintain consistency with. It requires you, as a busy parent, to be placed in a timeout of sorts as well. You have to make sure they are sitting where you told them to sit, and to stay silent if you have told them to stay silent. You don't have the luxury of getting on the phone or going about other tasks because they need supervision during the timeout. For the child, it creates an opportunity for bitterness, self-pity, and defiance to creep in. The choice is yours. Choose wisely.

If you choose to spank, you need a clear, well-thought-out plan of what actions or attitudes will call for it. Consistency is key, and it can never be done out of anger. We limited spankings to lying, disobedience, and lack of respect toward us as parents. Just remember that correcting behavior, not punishing wrongs, is the goal.

Have you heard of Pavlov's Dog? Ivan Pavlov was a Russian psychologist who lived in the 1800s. He learned a form of behavior modification known today as classical conditioning. He had a dog that he observed while it ate. He noticed that the simple act of eating caused the dog to salivate. That's not unusual. In fact, it's what we do every time we eat. It's an unconditioned response. But, he noticed that the dog associated his assistant with food. Any time the assistant came in, whether with or without food, the dog would salivate. Pavlov became curious to know if other external factors could stimulate that same response. Was there a way another mechanism could be substituted to bring about the same response? He got a bell and rang it before placing the food in front of the dog. Sure enough, after several feedings, the dog began to salivate every time the bell rang, with or without placing food in front of him. He discovered classical conditioning. It is the fact that something neutral like a bell if associated closely with the giving of the food, created a conditioned response. Now, I know you're asking yourself, "what does this have to do with my child?"

When your child is doing a natural act of resistance, and you want it to stop, you can condition them in the same way as Pavlov did his dog. It is classical conditioning in reverse. They act out, you spank them soon after, and they associate the pain with the act. Since the pain is more painful than the pleasure found in acting out, they are conditioned not to act out.

We had a simple structure that worked for us. When one of our kids misbehaved in a serious way, we would send them to our bedroom. It was for us as much as for them. It gave us a chance to control our own emotions, and it gave them just a little time to let healthy fear do its thing. Then we would listen to them. At this point, we would decide whether spanking was appropriate or if reasoned conversation was sufficient. We would then affirm our love for them, give them a hug, and pray together.

Paul David Tripp, a pastor, and author writing on this subject suggests a series of questions that helps a child discover for himself how to make better choices.[13] Imagine that just as you walk into the room where your children are, you see one of them throw a toy at the other one. You sit them down and ask them this series of questions:

1. What was going on?

   You ask questions, getting the child to tell you their version. You're not lecturing but listening. You're looking for them to reveal their heart. You're asking questions the child could never ask themselves.

2. What were you thinking and feeling as it was happening?

   You're getting them to reveal their heart. That is the goal. The heart is what controls our behavior.

3. What did you do in response?

   We want them to see that they weren't responding to the situation, but how their heart felt during the situation. This gives insight to our child as to what is happening in their heart.

4. Why did you do it?

   We want them to see what their motive was to do what they did. We are helping them understand that their behavior flows from the thoughts and desires of the heart. Wrong thoughts, wrong desires, lead to wrong behavior. (Hebrews 4:12)

5. What was the result?

   We are getting them to own the harvest of what they sowed.

The goal is to ask kids questions that stir a conversation they could never have by themselves. The goal is that they learn over the years to do this themselves. We call it "Self-talk."

Whatever method you choose, remember, if you put off discipline, problems compound. There is an old saying, "You reap what you sow." Give them everything they want, let them have their way, and you will reap an ungrateful child. Give a child free reign and let them tear things up and make excuses for them, and you will raise a child with no order, always making excuses.

Find the balance that works for you. Don't grow weary in doing this. You will reap blessings down the road.

CHAPTER TWELVE

KIDS ARE FRAGILE

The Golden Rule is Your Measuring Stick

Jesus was an incredible teacher and mentor. His strength was that He was deeply in love with His followers. He treated them with value. He loved them. They knew they could trust Him. There was a time when Jesus was teaching to a large crowd, and some were struggling with His message and quit following Him. Even those close to Him said, "This is hard teaching." He looked at them and replied, "Do you want to leave too?" I love Peter's response. He loved Jesus fully. He said, "Lord, who else would we follow. You have words of life!" Don't you love that!

We learn best from those we love most. If we want to impact our kids, we have to love them fully. More importantly, they have to know it. There is an old adage that says, "more is caught than taught." How we live our lives is more important than what we say. There is a sobering truth that the Apostle Paul gave to his young friend, Timothy. He said, "Watch how you live and what you say because you will save not just yourself but those who follow you."

It is crucial to keep that at the forefront of your mind that *kids are people too*. They are fragile emotionally. They have feelings. Everything you say to them, everything you do to and with them, should be filtered through the golden rule. "Do to others what you would have them do to you." The question that we should ask ourselves before we are tempted to discipline our children is, "If the tables were turned, is this how I would want to be treated?" Seriously. Think about it. Do you like being yelled at by someone? Do you like to be called out in front of everyone for a wrong you did? Do you like to be told, "You're stupid!" or, "You make me so mad!" Why do we think it's okay to treat or talk to our children that way?

You are the lead change agent in your child's life. They need to see grace and love in action in everything you do. Don't allow your emotions to control how you respond to what they do. The first six years will test everything in you. It will test your stamina, your determination, your resolve. You cannot allow your "bad day" to be an excuse for how you treat your children.

Your children hear the things you say about them. Be careful. They will live up to how you label them. When you tell others, "She's my little drama queen," or, "He's my ADHD little brat," or, "They're my little worrywarts," you are giving them a label that they don't need. Just because they did something stupid doesn't give you the right to say, "you're so stupid!" It is, on occasion, necessary to say that they are being foolish, but not that they are a fool. Do you see the difference?

One label defines the act. The other defines them. What they did may have been foolish, but they are not foolish.

Your toddler and preschooler are children. They will do childish things. They will spill the milk. They will break valuable things. They will be loud and nagging. Those are childish things. Lead them in love. We have to know the difference between childishness and rebellion. At this stage of their life, we are focusing on rebellion. Give them much grace with childishness. Be patient. Rebellion is what we have to deal with, but even that is to be done with grace. Our goal isn't perfection; it's growth.

When we lead our children to become self-controlled, we cannot do so out of anger or embarrassment, or from our own control issues. Again, the golden rule must become a part of our DNA. Treat them with dignity. When you discipline them, do so in private. My heart always hurts when I am with parents, and they begin to lecture or threaten their children in front of everyone. That kind of activity breaks their spirit, not their will. What your child thinks of you is way more important than what your guests or friends looking on, feel about you!

The words of Solomon always rang in my ears when I interacted with my kids, and it does so even as they are grown. It is this, "Above all else, guard your heart, for everything you do flows from it."[14] It is our role at this point in our children's lives to guard their hearts while they are learning how to defend it themselves. Hearts can be cold or warm, hard or tender, brave or fearful, broken or mended. Remember, we are not merely after behavior modification. We are molding their hearts.

There is a deep desire in every one of us to know and to be known—to love and be loved. Security comes from these truths. When we are fully known and loved anyway, there is unimaginable security that is nurtured in us. Kids want to know that they matter, that they fit in, that they belong, and that they are loved. It is our job to pave the way to see that security is planted in them, that it is watered by constant reaffirmation, and that the fruit of that security is a person who is free to love others fully.

There are a couple more practical needs that we all crave. We all want attention, and we all want to feel in control of our lives. When these felt needs go unmet, kids will act out to get them. These two needs are always at play in the background. The temper tantrums, the whining, the constant nagging while you are on the phone or trying to work, are in many instances, the child crying out for attention or control.

It is essential at this phase to understand how to meet that need and in some ways, calm them down. It's what we call "parent-time," or PTs for short. At least two times a day, get down on their level, look them in the eye, and say, "I've got about ten minutes of free time. What would you like to do together?" This, done consistently, will meet their need for attention.

As for control, give them choices. Instead of laying out what they are going to wear the next day, bring them into the decision making. Give them a couple of options. It's the same with food. Don't simply fill their plate. Ask them if they would rather have carrots, peas, or both. You have controlled the choices, but they will feel more like they have freedom. When kids think they have a choice and that they have your attention, behavior improves significantly. You will be amazed at the difference these action steps make in your child's overall behavior.

CHAPTER THIRTEEN
REVERSE ENGINEERING THE K-5 GRADUATE

Sketching out what your first grader will look like

Tammy and I have been sketching out various floor plans for a carriage house. Building something to live in that is half the size of what we've lived in for the past thirty years requires focusing on the essentials. A walk-in closet is awesome to have until you have to choose between it or a small guest room. Should we have one large bathroom for everything, or a small full bath and a separate half-bath? Downsizing forces you to prioritize the essentials.

It is the same when we sketch a blueprint for what we would like our children to look like as they head into elementary school. When we look at the newborn to six-year-old phase, the discipline phase, we need to choose the essential qualities and values that we want to see developed during those years. Grab your journal and let's start dreaming together about what your child will look like as they reach that milestone of six years old.

If your child is already beyond the six-year-old milestone, don't simply rush past this. Use this as a way of evaluating where your child is presently in light of this phase. For those who have a child in this phase, let's get to work. Imagine that child of yours in a few different scenarios; scenes like, how they will interact with new friends, how they will respond to their teacher, how they will handle someone being mean to them, what they will do when a teacher is correcting them, or how they will react to someone else being mistreated. Will they pay attention and listen? What will their study habits be? Will they see the glass as half-full or half-empty? You get the idea. Just create different scenes. The more, the better. You are trying to anticipate your child in real life scenarios and envision how you would like them to respond to life as it comes at them.

At the risk of being redundant, let's remember that what others see is the behavior of our child—how they act and respond to life as it happens to them. But the unseen attitude is where that behavior comes from. All behavior flows from the attitudes of the heart. Behind every act, every behavior seen is an attitude of the heart being revealed. Attitudes are the viewpoint from which we see life. There are pessimistic attitudes, optimistic attitudes, selfish attitudes, selfless attitudes, loving attitudes, and hateful attitudes. Attitudes flow from a healthy self-esteem or unhealthy self-esteem, a generous attitude, or a hoarding attitude. These attitudes come from somewhere. They didn't just randomly appear. If we can shape the attitude, we can alter the behavior.

Attitudes flow from the heart. The heart is always thinking and always wanting. The heart is shaped by what we believe. Thought is the brain processing a set of truths. Not all of our beliefs are true. Take, for instance, the concept of fairness. We crave that others will be fair to us. We are less concerned that we are fair to others, but that is human nature. But our mind has this thought about fairness running in the background. When we are treated with what we perceive to be an unfair act, our attitude processes that scene, it wants fairness, and our behavior screams out, "No Fair!" We all know life isn't fair, but until we know that instinctively, we will always react to unfairness in a victim-like, selfish way.

Truth matters. Truth is tricky. We can all be deceived about what is true and what isn't. Just because life should be fair doesn't mean it is. Solomon says, "As a person thinks in their heart, so are they." If we can direct the thoughts of our children, we can shape their attitudes, which will alter their behavior.

Now, keeping that in mind, let's focus on the values or principles that we want to see in our six-year-old. You can list as many as you like, but for our purpose here, let's focus on a few of the essentials. Too many and we will get bogged down. We wanted our kids at this phase to be loving, respectful, obedient, self-controlled, grateful, and truthful. If those are the behavioral traits, then I needed to see to it that I encouraged a set of truths and nurtured them into my kids' mind. It starts by briefly defining each value.

What does it mean to be loving? I am loving when I treat other people the way I want to be treated. My grandson, Eli, is nine years old. He saw a classmate getting ridiculed at school this week because he brought his lunch to school in a brown paper sack. In frustration, the boy threw his food in the trash. Eli noticed it, got in line, bought the boy a lunch, and sat down with him. A teacher saw what Eli did and told his mother. That made me one proud Poppy. That behavior flowed from an attitude that was nurtured in his heart. How do we instill that in our child? Those behaviors are the result of being directional and intentional about teaching love.

What does it mean to be respectful? I am respectful when I value someone as important as I want to be valued. I wanted my kids to treat everyone as important. Everyone matters. It doesn't matter their color, weight, clothing styles, or financial standing. I wanted them to say, "Yes ma'am" and "No ma'am," "Yes sir" and "No sir" to every adult. I wanted them to look people in the eye when being spoken to. We used to call behavior like this "manners." Saying things, like "please" and "thank you" instinctively is a sign of a respectful child. Respect means being considerate of others as well. Little things like teaching your son not to burp or poot in front of girls, or anyone for that matter. These things don't just happen; it is the result of parents being proactive and direct.

What does it mean to be obedient? I am obedient when I comply with rules that help create order. Few things are more frustrating to watch than a child who won't obey those in authority. You've been in that situation. A parent tells their child to stop running, and the child continues to run. Then they say, "It's time to go, let's pick up the toys!" and the parent is ignored. A teacher tells the kids to get in line, and nothing happens. Now, I'm not the best rule keeper. I'm a rebel at heart, but obedience is essential at this phase in a child's life. It sets boundaries, creates order, and establishes a sense of peace.

What does it mean to be self-controlled? I am self-controlled when I don't allow my emotions to overrule my values. Watching a child throw a temper tantrum or cry uncontrollably when they don't get their way is a sign of a child that lacks self-control. Without self-control, things like anger, bitterness, and violence will show up in behavior. A sign of maturity is when kids behave without being told to do so. There are few things we can truly control in this life, but every child needs to learn to control their emotions.

What does it mean to be grateful? I am grateful when I acknowledge the little acts of kindness that others do for me. Gratefulness is an amazingly powerful value that keeps jealousy, envy, and greed from eating us alive. It brings optimism and contentment that is attractive. It prevents entitlement from taking root. The overabundance of toys and gadgets that kids receive these days is destroying the opportunity to instill thankfulness in their hearts. But, when a child is grateful for little things, like an act of service, clean clothes, or food on the table, you will enjoy a home at peace.

What does it mean to be truthful? I am truthful when I am honest about my actions, feelings, and thoughts. When we are self-deceived, or we seek to deceive others, relationships cease to exist. Trust is the key to relationships. Where lying exists, progress in relationships cannot happen.

Once the values are cemented in our brain, everything else is about reinforcing and encouraging those behaviors. The home is the training ground of kids. It is where much of their character and attitude will be shaped. Kids will learn truths from the behavior of others and the information fed to them and processed in their brain. In the next chapter, we will discuss the best way for this to happen.

CHAPTER FOURTEEN

FINDING QUALITY TIME IN THE ROUTINE OF LIFE

Rethinking morning, meals, & bedtime routines

There was a point, early in our marriage, when we had three kids four years of age and under. Tammy was a busy stay-at-home mom, and I was focused on doing student ministry and getting my college degree. We were busy in those days. I was up late every night with different student groups. I would be up early studying theology and Greek. There were classes, staff meetings, counseling appointments, and lots of interaction with students by way of hiking, sporting events, lunch at various high schools, teaching Bible at the local Christian school, and hanging out in fast food joints. I never took a day off. I didn't have a great deal of time to spend with my kids, or Tammy for that matter. Tammy was also involved in our student ministry. She attended our junior high meetings on Sundays. The college students met in our home on Tuesday evenings, and we had senior high school meetings on Wednesday. Most of those nights she would break away at some point and get the kids ready for bed—changing diapers, brushing teeth, getting water, tucking them in, praying with them, and answering the endless questions of toddlers.

I remember the time we had "the talk." Tammy is not the emotionally driven type of person who is constantly nagging or fussing at me about what I'm doing or not doing as a husband or father. So, when she is sitting on the sofa waiting on me as I come through the door, I know a serious conversation is about to happen. I'm a people-pleaser at heart, so I tense up like a kid being called to the principal's office when I see her sitting there. The conversation that followed was monumental and life-changing for my family and me. It was hard for her to have "the talk."

When you're married to a pastor, and you want to tell him he's working too much, you feel as though you are preventing someone from doing "God's work." She told me she felt overwhelmed taking care of the kids by herself. "Your kids need some of the attention you are giving everyone else's kids," she said. Something had to give. She was at the end of her rope, hanging on by a thread. I had been so busy; I didn't even see it. I started taking Fridays off. We went to the park, rode paddle boats around the lake, and rode bikes. We started eating dinner together as a family every night. I even started telling bedtime stories. That "talk" was transformational. I'm embarrassed that I was so imbalanced in those days but grateful for my wife for the honesty and resolve she has.

The challenge was to find more time to spend with the kids in meaningful ways. What we discovered is that you can't plan quality time. It's not merely a switch you flip, and the magic moments happen. The reason why gold is valuable is because it's not readily found lying around. You don't simply plant and water and wait for gold to grow. It is found as you spend time dipping a pan into the river and sifting out the rocks to see if there is a hint of gold. Somewhere in all of that "panning," you discover the "good stuff."

It's true of diamonds as well. There is a little research that happens, and then mines are dug, clutter and dirt are moved, and then after a bit of time, the magic is found. After a time, treasure seekers begin to discover the secrets and signs to make it a little more predictable as to where the treasure will be found.

Finding those magical moments with our kids happens similarly. We start spending time interacting with them in their world, and we show them a glimpse of our world. We spend quantity time with them and in the doing of that, the magic of quality time shows up. Those moments when our child is learning, trust is developing, and essential values for living are found.

We discovered along the way that there are certain times throughout the day when quality time seemed to show up more frequently. These times are easy to miss because, at first glance, they seem to be routine moments in the day. But if we are proactive and directional in those moments, magic happens. The moments to focus on and to be intentional about, happen at mealtimes, bedtimes, morning time, and nap or quiet times. Focus on these, prepare for these, be proactive and directional about these, and you will discover incredible opportunities to shape the heart of your child so that the values you set in your Directional Parenting Blueprint will be developed.

Bedtime Routine

Let's start with the bedtime routine. It is usually the easiest one to start and do consistently. It isn't the time to rush everybody up to bed so you can get back to watching your TV shows, check social media, or whatever your favorite night time pleasures are. Bedtime can be a little crazy. There are toys to put away, teeth that need to be brushed, and stuffed animals, blankets, or their favorite cuddle items that need to be gathered. There is that one thing they need to tell you that turns into countless "one more thing" to say. Most of you can relate. For too many parents, this feels like a chore. They get frustrated because it's taking the kids too long in the bathroom. They think they are stalling and being defiant. The yelling begins. The threats of what will happen if they get out of bed one more time. The kids are upset, the parent is frustrated, and a valuable opportunity is wasted. The last thing that happens in the day for you and your child shouldn't be harsh, stern, angry, or frustrating.

It is a time when the child is vulnerable. Children get scared. They want to talk. They want to listen. They want to be cuddled. It is one of the best times to plant values into them. What our conscious mind thinks about right before we go to bed is what our subconscious mind processes while we sleep. It should be a pleasant, enjoyable moment in your child's day. The key to it all is your mindset. You set the tone. Work on getting better at this routine.

It is important that all the prep work of getting ready for bed happens. After the teeth are brushed, the pajamas are on, the cuddle buddies are nestled in, and the glass of water is on the bedside table, either lay in their bed with them or sit in a chair beside them and let the magic begin.

There are several components to what happens during this special time. Books are read, stories are told, highs and lows of the day are shared, prayers are said, along with lots of hugs and kisses. Not all of these will necessarily happen every night, but a combination of some of these should. Every night, we prayed, and we always gave lots of hugs and kisses. Books, stories, and conversations were interchanged from night to night. It's important to end the routine with the prayer, hugs, and kisses. The power of those actions cements two truths in their minds. That they are watched over, and they are loved. It builds a sense of belonging and security that will pay huge dividends throughout the parenting years.

Because our subconscious mind processes the last things our conscious mind focuses on during sleep, the bedtime flow is the perfect time to focus on values. In ancient days, before print or paper, the telling and retelling of stories were how knowledge, wisdom, logic, values, and life lessons were handed down. Do your research but look for children's books that reinforce the values of respect, obedience, self-control, gratefulness, honesty, love, and service. Save the fun and goofy books for another time. Directional, proactive parenting will mean you stay focused on planting seeds of healthy values in them before bed. Aesop's Fables are full of short, rich stories from the animal world. Try Dr. Seuss, *Did I Ever Tell You How Lucky You Are*, on gratitude. *The Little Red Hen* is a classic for teaching about selfishness. *The Berenstain Bears and the Truth*, *The Giving Tree*, Ken Gire's *Adventures in the Big Thicket*, and, my book, Uncle Poppy's *Sandy the Selfish Seagull*, are some books to get you started. Don't just look for popular books. Take the road less traveled. Get off the beaten path and saturate your child's mind and yours with valuable lessons and reminders.

Real stories from your childhood and those of real people in history are powerful. Sometimes, the stories come to us in the moment, but it is helpful to find some time to reflect on your childhood about each of the values you desire in your child and how you learned the benefits of those values yourself. Get a notebook to categorize and log stories as they come to mind. Who knows, you might just become a storyteller and turn those into a book yourself someday. Bible stories provide a solid foundation for teaching values as well.

Books and stories will help open the door to naturally discuss recent failures and successes that you and your children have had. It's a place for reflection, confession, goal-setting, and resolve to be better.

End those times with prayers. Teach them by example. You pray and then teach them to pray. Give hugs, kisses, and look them in the eye and tell them you love them, and you always will. I'm telling you; this little routine can change the course of your life, their lives, and those that come into their lives in the future.

Morning Routine

Focusing on mindset and attitude each morning will affect how our day goes as well as those who interact with us. The same goes for our kids. It is usually one of the more chaotic times of the day. If you are the type of parent who always feels rushed and frantic in the mornings, set your alarm for thirty minutes earlier than normal. No, seriously. I'm not kidding here. Put the book down and go do it now. We'll wait for you. Okay,

I'm kidding sort of, but not about setting your alarm for thirty minutes earlier than usual. Just do it and get used to getting up earlier. Those extra thirty minutes will allow for a little less *chaos*, and a lot more *calm*.

The opportunities provided by this routine depend on the age of your child and whether you are a stay-at-home or work-from-home parent. How we wake our children at this phase is important. Just remember the golden rule. If you don't want to be startled awake or yelled at for not getting up when told, then don't do that to them. If they are old enough to dress themselves, give them a few choices of clothes and let them do the rest. Remember, giving them choices is crucial. To teach them discipline, get them to make their bed. Making their bed teaches them responsibility. It gives them a task that they can quickly conquer and sets up the day for success. I love this quote from Admiral William H. McRaven:

> If you want to change the world, start off by making your bed. If you make your bed every morning, you will have accomplished the first task of the day. It will give you a small sense of pride, and it will encourage you to do another task, and another, and another. And by the end of the day, that one task completed will have turned into many tasks completed. Making your bed will also reinforce the fact that the little things in life matter. If you can't do the little things right, you'll never be able to do the big things right. And, if by chance you have a miserable day, you will come home to a bed that is made; that you made. And, a made bed gives you encouragement that tomorrow will be better. [15]

Not everyone will be able to eat breakfast together, but if it's possible, then do it. It will reinforce the values that we'll take a look at in the mealtime routine. Before everyone rushes out the door, gather the family into your favorite room or around the kitchen table. It is like the pre-game speech given before the big game. Remind your kids of your family values. You may want to put them down into a mission statement at some point. But focus on at least one value a day. Read from a Bible devotional book for kids, and pray over them. The morning routine is not the time to fight or bring up negative issues. Look them in the eye, tell them you love them, that you are for them, and that nothing they do today could make you not love them. Give them a big hug. Those last words you utter to them, whether they are going to daycare or preschool, will help them when life gets tough for them there.

Remember that it is these little things, planted and watered consistently over long periods, that will produce a harvest of the values that you want to see developed in your child's life. We will truly reap what we sow. As the Apostle Paul says, "So let's not get tired of doing what is good. At just the right time, we will reap a harvest of blessing if we don't give up."[17]

Playtime Routine

Few things shape the imagination and critical thinking skills of a preschooler more than good, healthy playing. The temptation today is to put a child in front of a TV, game box, or tablet, and keep them busy. Again, you are a proactive parent. You have decided to take action and are shaping your child in a specific direction. While there are times that technology is good and healthy for our children, playtime is not that time. This is the time to give them as much sensory stimulation as possible, cause questions to arise, and the imagination to be challenged.

When we moved into our home out in the woods, we had this spot right off our patio that wouldn't grow any grass. Being a creative type, I dug out the area, built a seawall against the embankment, a boardwalk on the other side, and filled it in with sand. We called it "Poppy's Beach." Because woods surrounded us, my backyard was filled with all kinds of critters. It proved to be an amazing place for our grandkids and friends as we gathered. Kids spent hours out there creating everything from race tracks and battlefields to castles. We hunted for lizards, ran the trails that I built up into the woods, and raced sticks along the little spring-fed creek down the hill. We even took walks down the old country lane to see Mikey, our neighbor's donkey. Now, I realize not all of you live in a place where that can happen. But you might consider putting up a treehouse or playhouse. The point is to get kids outside and let them get their hands dirty, their imagination flowing, and their sense of wonder developing.

Be a minimalist when it comes to toys. Too many toys create an opportunity to be less grateful. We encourage young parents to put half of the toys away somewhere, then maybe do it again, depending on the amount. What's left should be a few of their child's favorite toys. Let them play with those. And when you sense that they are tired of them, swap them out with some of the toys you had put away. In effect, you're creating a lending library of sorts for your kids. The temptation to buy every new shiny thing that comes along is real. Don't fall for it. Too much stuff will contribute to a short attention span, a sense of entitlement, greed, and as we said earlier, a lack of gratefulness.

The brain of a child in the discipline phase is learning at the fastest rate they will experience over their entire life. Be careful not to waste the opportunity by merely handing them gadgets. While there is a place for those things, nothing compares to the simplicity of imagination.

Playtime, when friends are around, allows you to teach the value of sharing, apply the golden rule, and teach the art of getting along with others.

Quiet Time Routine

This might be the most challenging to get going. Quiet time is essential, but unlike us adults who would love a quiet time, few kids readily look forward to it. The quiet time is not nap time, though a child should be free to do so. It is a time for them to look at books or learn how to color or scribble on a notepad. Let them listen to music. It is an opportunity for them to learn to sit still and to develop discipline. It is a time when study habits are subtly being formed.

It may only last for five minutes, or it may last for thirty. It may involve you sitting on the couch with them, holding them and sharing your childhood memories with them, or talking about the book that was read at bedtime. The possibilities are endless.

Mealtime Routine

This has always been one of my favorite times of the day. Not merely because I love to eat, which is true, but because it is like a mini celebration. For most of us, Thanksgiving, Christmas, Easter, Memorial Day, 4th of July, Labor Day, and birthdays, involve food. Just bring up the name of one of the holidays, and certain foods come to mind. Food is life. Solomon said, "There is nothing better under the sun than to eat, drink, and be glad."[17] Whether it is a noon-time meal or evening dinner, get in the habit of gathering the whole family around a table at least once a day if possible.

Too many families neglect to see the potential value in this daily act. For most, it becomes about stuffing food in and getting on with life. It's become routine to plop down in front of the TV with a plate in hand and check out. Proactive parents are wise enough to see the golden opportunity for rich, valuable moments to shape their children and enjoy the mini celebration of life.

My dad built a little "Bama table" for my sister when she went off to college. It was built to slide under a dorm bed. She would pull it out so her and her roommate and others could sit on the floor around it and enjoy a meal together. We called it the "Bama table" because she went to the University of Alabama and Dad painted it white, put Crimson Tide decals all over it, and added a coat of varnish on top. Somehow, I inherited that table, and when our kids were small, we would set that table up, sit around it, and enjoy a meal. My grandkids sit around it today. The memories of that table still fill my heart.

For the discipline phase, the value of the table is to teach manners, respect, gratefulness, and discipline. It might just be the greatest teaching moment of all the routines. As we gathered, we always thanked the one who provided the meal, whether prepared or bought. It teaches respect. We prayed before every meal and often read a Bible verse from a stack of memory cards that sat on our table. This taught our kids how to pray and to be grateful for the daily things. While we ate, we talked about the day, the highs and lows, the new things learned, and stories of the day shared. We taught how to use forks and spoons, how to eat with your mouth closed, to not talk with your mouth full, to learn to pass the food around, to wipe our mouths, to put the dishes away, to ask to be excused, and to say thank you to the cook. We practiced table manners and then rewarded our kids by going out to eat on occasion so they could practice in public. The benefit was that our meals out were less embarrassing, chaotic, and frustrating.

As you read this section, it can be a little overwhelming. You may be thinking, *this is too much work—too much preparation. I don't have time for this.* Don't stress over it. Begin small, and implement one routine, and then another, until they are consistently a part of your family's DNA. You may not be able to do each of them every day. Just get in the habit of allowing these routines to be the place where values are easily instilled. There will be challenges. The younger the child, the less complicated the times will be. The more children, the more challenging, because of the age differences. The important thing is to get started, use your creativity and style to build a rich heritage, and create kids who you like to be around, who others like to be around, and who like themselves.

CHAPTER FIFTEEN
RANDY'S DISCIPLINE RANTS

Just my perspective on raising toddlers

Before we close out this section covering the Discipline Phase, I have a few thoughts that I am passionate about. These are lessons and tips about things that aren't easily seen while you are in the moment. You may think of them after the Discipline Phase has come and gone. They are things you see out of life's rearview mirror. Some of these may come instinctively to you, but I've seen too many parents miss these principles or truths.

We could call this a rant, or impassioned ramblings. I prefer to call it "sagacity." Sagacity, which is really common sense, or keen observation about practical life, is sometimes missed in the heat of the moment. Some of these things, you may take exception to or disagree with. You may even get offended by them. I hope they challenge you and make you better prepared for the moment. These are meant to spare you potential regret and frustration as you move along this spectrum of parenting. These aren't in any particular order—just random things I need to say. You ready?

If you are a married couple raising kids together, don't let your kids come between you. You are a team. Stick together. Kids are smart. They instinctively know how to find the weak link, how to get their way, and how to manipulate you. Make a commitment to lock arms and stand together. Don't talk to your child about your spouse in a negative way. Don't make them choose a side. Never argue in front of your kids. It is even more critical if you are divorced, and the child is moving back and forth between homes.

Avoid letting your kids become the priority. Don't let your home become child-centered. The health of your marriage is important. Don't feel guilty having time for just the two of you. The kids don't have to stay up as late as you do. Don't let them guilt you into that. And *do not* let your kids sleep in the same bed as you. Don't do it! If you ever start it, it will be a fight to undo it.

Stop giving your child every shiny object that comes along. It is destructive in so many ways. Quit seeing who can throw the biggest birthday celebration. Don't bow to that pressure. It is a potential landmine that will breed an unhealthy entitlement mentality into your child. It's okay to have a small intimate party with only a few gifts. To constantly throw gifts at them may make you feel better, but it's not helping your child. What they really want is *you*!

Life is not fair! Don't obsess over that. Everything is not solved by fairness. You need to learn that life will come at you harder than other parents sometimes, and your kids need to learn to be content with what they have. Contentment is huge. The earlier it can be developed, the better for all.

Keep your home clean and neat. Don't be that home where toys are all over the floor—cups and plates are on every coffee table and end table in the house. Don't make excuses for it. Just keep it neat and clean. Model it for your kids.

Stop making excuses for your child's misbehavior. Being tired is not the only reason why children act out. They will hear you say it and will use it to justify their actions. When you or I are tired, we don't get away with that as an excuse for acting out. We say that many times to let ourselves off the hook while dealing with the situation.

Surround yourself with other parents who share your values. It will make parenting easier. Gather your friends, get them to read this book, and have a healthy dialogue.

Kids are only little once. These first six years are so vital for their future, and yours as well. Don't rush to put them in daycare or preschool. I know for many of you, both parents are working. But figure out how to live on less, work from home, or put your career on hold. You do not want to entrust this valuable time to others. If childcare is necessary, then choose wisely. There are thousands of reasons why this isn't practical, but there are a few very good reasons why you should figure it out—your kids!

Gather advice from others but listen carefully to your own voice. Your heart desires things—intuitively knows things. Don't let others crowd your voice out. Educators will strong arm you and scare you into submission. It's okay to be a rebel. You choose whether you want to put your child in public school, private school, or home school. You have to listen to your heart. These are your babies! Doctors will tell you your child needs this treatment or that prescription. Again, listen to your heart. Friends who have no kids or who have raised kids that you don't want yours to grow up to be like, will give you advice. Listen, but again, listen to your own heart above all.

See, that wasn't so bad. Feel free to disagree with me. I still love you and believe in you. It's good that we have differing opinions. It challenges us to change or gives us confirmation that we are on the right track. Both are good.

PART FOUR
HAVING FUN WITH THE GRADE-SCHOOLER IN THE TRAINING PHASE

Here is where we begin to help our child discover their unique personality. You will learn how to shape and train them in how life is best lived by helping them understand key traits and beliefs that will help them to navigate their world.

CHAPTER SIXTEEN

BRING ON THE CHOICES

Giving kids choices helps them learn to mature

First grade was a big deal when I was growing up. None of my classmates went to kindergarten. First grade was the first time I was put into an organized group of kids the same age as me. Well, except for that time my parents took me to a Sunday school class when I was four or five. So, unless you went to church, this was a new and strange experience. I was one of the thirty-seven students in Miss Russell's class—eighteen boys and nineteen girls. I spent the next few years growing to adolescence with most of these kids. They became my friends, classmates, and playmates. Over those years, these friends of mine, along with the teachers, my parents, and my family, shaped who I would be when I entered high school.

Your children in this training phase right now are filled with friendships and are trying to figure out how that works. School is a bit more serious and maybe a bit more of a challenge than it used to be. The world view they are developing is being tested as well as their values. Their personalities are becoming more visible and clearly defined. It is an incredible time as a parent. We have laid the foundation of discipline, and we now build on it by training them how to be proactive in their response to life and to have a healthy and wise reaction to what comes their way.

By training, we mean that they should be learning how to make more of the choices throughout the day. As parents, we should be more conscious about helping them understand the "why" behind what we are asking them to do. The phrase, "Because I said so!" may get them to do what you want, but it's not training them how to respond to life. Life isn't simply about following orders from those in authority. Life is experienced best when a set of values and principles become the truths that we view the world through. It is what we want for our kids. Values and principles will live in them long after the "because I said so," will.

The mistake many parents make is in believing that outward performance equals core values. But that is not necessarily true. It's like the little boy who was standing up in class when the teacher told him to sit down. He refused at first, and then with threats of a visit to the principle, he finally sat down. But he mumbled under his breath, "I'm sitting down on the outside, but I'm still standing on the inside."

While we can make our children perform and behave outwardly in a certain way, and sometimes that's necessary, the goal in the training phase is to help them see and embrace a set of values and principles that will guide them well after they have moved into adulthood. The privilege of a parent is that we get to shape much of what they value. It should make every parent put the brakes on and begin to ask themselves what their own core values and principles are. Most of us never take the time to examine what we believe about God, others, ourselves, and how those relationships function on a day to day basis. We will take a look at the *what* and the *how* in the following chapters.

It's possible that our child's need for attention and control are not getting met while at school. This means those parent times (PTs) are essential. They need those hugs, back rubs, wrestling, and hair brushing. They need increased responsibility in a way that gives them a measure of control, so choices and chores can't be neglected. They should be given more choice about what style of clothes to wear, whether they will do their homework right after school or should they relax a bit first. They will begin choosing the style of music that speaks to them and what books they want to read. For that, they may need a little training to see the importance of good books and the enjoyment of reading.

Responsibility can also come by turning over the act of getting their lunches together, changing the sheets on their bed, neatly folding clothes and keeping them in order, deciding what needs to be hung up, and what gets put in drawers. They should know how to wash clothes, how to set the table, how to clear the table, load the dishwasher, or hand wash the dishes.

As they mature through this training phase, they will learn to cook and discover what a healthy balanced diet is. They will learn the difference between straightening a room and cleaning a room, or how to rake leaves. Chores used as a teaching and training tool will serve them well throughout their lives. Again, it is important to explain the "why" behind the "what." This essential step, the art of training by explaining the "why" will create a willingness on their part to begin to do the necessary chores in a more consistent and better manner than their friends—by choosing to instill choice and responsibilities.

It won't be easy. You should anticipate resistance to the idea of work, chores, and responsibilities. Power struggles will come. They will want to negotiate with you, which isn't a bad thing. Life is full of negotiating, so it is better that they learn how from you than from the world. Don't look at their desire to negotiate as rebellion. Not everything is negotiable, but when it is appropriate, it's healthy.

When they misbehave, become rebellious, or defiant, we have to be prepared. For most parents, this becomes a battleground, but it doesn't have to be. Be proactive here. Anticipate what you will do. If you chose to spank, then by this time, that response should be rare, if ever. Grounding them will create an opportunity for bitterness to creep in. Taking away privileges will have the same effect. While there are times for punishment, and when those times come, the child should know exactly the "why" behind the "what" concerning the punishment. Most parents punish out of their own frustration. We can't react rashly every time the child doesn't do "right." Yelling and arguing have no place in training. You are the parent. Be slow in bringing the hammer down. Your attitude is essential—more so than their action.

There are a couple of more productive options when we see defiance and too much push back coming from our kids. One is what is known as "When/ Then" and the other is "Either/Or." Get these in your parenting DNA. These options will be invaluable to you as well as to them. "When/Then" is giving them responsibility by giving them a choice in the situation. Imagine they haven't straightened their room, or they haven't done what you asked them to do, and you see that they are doing something else. You remind them of the responsibility that needs attention, and then you say, "When you straighten up your room, then you can go outside and play." They may respond, by saying, "But, Mom, I'm in the middle of a game." You can allow for negotiations, or you can say, "I'm sorry, but when you straighten your room, then you can finish your game." At that point, negotiations are over, hopefully without unhealthy confrontation.

If "When/Then" didn't get them to take responsibility, then you apply the "Either/Or" tactic. You'll say something like, "Either you straighten your room, or you won't play the game at all today." It is the line in the sand. It should rarely be the first choice. "When/Then" is the best choice and the "Either/Or" is your next move. If this is done consistently, you will successfully train your kids in responsibility and accountability. That is a parenting win!

You should avoid bribing or rewarding them at all cost for doing what they should be doing. Bribes and rewards don't help them to cement values and principles in their lives. The motivation to do right should not come from an outward reward, but an inner conviction. Rewards do have their place, like when they read that extra book, or you witnessed them doing the right thing without you telling them, and you want to encourage them to continue doing those things through positive reinforcement. We celebrate wins, like when they have set a goal to raise money for a friend's need, or they hit a weight loss goal. This is when a reward helps drive core values in them.

CHAPTER SEVENTEEN

CRANK UP THE LOVE

Learning to speak their love language

I was blessed with great parents. My dad always anticipated my needs and met them without me even having to ask. When he saw me trying to gain weight as a skinny kid, he had his fabrication shop build me a weight bench that he designed. When I needed a car, he got a '68 Mustang and restored it for me. When my kids came along, he paid for braces for each one. He never stopped giving to me 'til the day he died. He loved meeting the needs of his family. My mom was always the cheerleader. Every word she uttered was filled with hope and love. She made me believe I could do anything. At eighty-nine years of age, she still tells me how handsome I am, or how proud she is of me. My mental and emotional stability has always been strong, and most of that is due to the undying love my parents showered on me by loving me well.

Good parenting is about influence. We are shaping our kids' thoughts, perspectives, attitudes, and in some ways, their behavior. The healthier we are in those areas, the better the results will be. There will always be a level of resistance from our kids as we seek to mold and shape their worldview. Because our kids are like us and are prone toward selfishness, choosing to value others will not be easy. Getting them to believe they can be anything they want will not be easy. A willingness to allow others to change us and to influence us comes from knowing that those desiring to influence us and change us genuinely love us. We will either fill our children's love tank up, or we will spend time dealing with the fallout from not filling it up. Love will always win the day!

When it comes to parenting, love is the key to everything. Growing up is hard. One of the keys to raising kids who turn out right is to love them well. Each of us, our kids included, have a way we receive love best. Gary Chapman, in his classic book, *The five love languages*,[18] lays them out in a very practical way. He defines them as words of affirmation, quality time, receiving gifts, acts of service, and physical touch. When you discover each of your children's love languages, and you begin to speak it to them consistently, you will see your influence and their willingness to change grow exponentially. Creating a home filled with love that flows in a way that fills each other up, creates a powerfully secure and stable environment for the whole family to thrive.

How do we find out what our child's love language is? There are signs if we know what to look for. We usually give to others the love language that we desire. So, the key is to observe how they display their love to you. Let's take a moment and look at each one of the languages.

Touch:

Does your child come in from school looking for a hug? Do they ask you for a back rub or to scratch their back? Do they bring you a hairbrush and ask you to brush their hair? Do they come and sit close to you when watching a movie? If so, then touch is most likely how they give and receive love. When you are disciplining them, they will need a hug to reinforce in their hearts that you love them, and you are disciplining them because you love them. When you are correcting them or helping to shape their minds, and you want to speak words of wisdom to them, do it while you are brushing their hair or sitting close to them. My dad was a hugger. He would give you a tight hug whenever you were coming in or going out. You had to brace yourself to avoid a cracked rib! When my kids came along, they began to call these hugs, "Grandandy hugs." Even after Grandandy passed away, and they have grown into adults with kids of their own, they often think back on those hugs with great comfort.

Gift-giving / Acts of Service:

Does your child bring you things like flowers or artwork? Do they clean their room or complete some other chore and want you to come and see what they have done? Do they do things for you that they think is important to you? When out shopping, do they see things and want to give them to their siblings or spouse? If you see these things, they most likely speak the language of gifts and acts of service. To keep their tank filled up, bring them a gift occasionally for no reason. Sit down and offer to help with their homework, or occasionally straighten their room for them. Never underestimate the impact of keeping their love tank filled. In the words of Mary Poppins, "It helps the medicine go down." During, or just after doing an act of service for them, is a great time to have a meaningful conversation.

Quality Time:

Are they asking to do things with you? Do they ask you to play with them? When you go to the store, do they ask to go? Do they want to do things with just you and not their brother or sister? If you have more than one in this age group, you have to plan individual time with each. And it's ok to give the older one different privileges than the younger ones. You have to be sensitive to the ones whose love language is quality time. It could be slipping off to the store, or a late-night snack to meet that craving they have for meaningful one-on-one time.

Words of Affirmation:

Are they telling you they love you at different times throughout the day? Do they say, "Mom, you sure are pretty!" or "Dad, you're strong!" Do they give you compliments? Do they say things like, "Did I do good?" Are they showing you their artwork or asking you to listen to them play their instrument? Words are powerful in shaping their inner voice. Words of affirmation give them a sense of security and belonging. Words show that their efforts haven't gone unnoticed, that they aren't invisible.

While my love language is touch, words of affirmation is my secondary. I never thought I needed encouragement from others until I encountered resistance from others. I need words of affirmation, even when my conscious thoughts tell me I don't.

There is a famous passage in the Bible that speaks about love, giving a grocery list of sorts, defining it. It's found in 1 Corinthians 13: 4-7:

"Love is patient, love is kind."
Breathe. Let them be little and always respond in kindness.

"It does not envy, it does not boast, it is not proud."
Don't always tell them you love them...show it!

"It does not dishonor others, it is not self-seeking, it is not easily angered, it keeps no record of wrongs."
Honor them, don't make their stuff about you. Keep calm, forgive.

"Love does not delight in evil but rejoices with the truth."
Love them, don't shame them when they confess their wrongs.

"It always protects, always trusts, always hopes, always perseveres."
Love always gives a covering of hope. Always.

"Love never fails."
Never, never, never give up loving them.

Go back and reread each of those phrases. It is the mindset that we, as parents, have to have if we are to influence our kids' lives. If we truly want to impact our kids, then we have to ensure that they know we love them. Just before this list of definitions of love in 1 Corinthians 13:1, are the words:

> If I speak in the tongues of men or of angels, but do not have love, I am only a resounding gong or a clanging cymbal.

If our kids lack confidence that we love them, our words are just noise! Let that sink in. Just because you're mad at your children at that moment, doesn't mean that you can withhold demonstrations of love. In fact, it is needed even more at those times.

Our kids need to know our love language as well. We should also help them to learn their siblings' love languages and practice loving well. Like all of us, they will do things that are unloving toward you or their siblings. That always needs to be addressed. Love never gets a day off. If they use negative, hurtful language, or they act selfishly, ask them, "Was that the loving thing to do?" We always appealed to the golden rule, and we still do today. I ask myself as well as my kids and grandkids to consider this question when conflict arises. "If the tables were turned, is this how I would want to be treated?" That one question brings emotion into the equation and takes the conversation to a much better end. Feelings and emotions will bring about transformation in a way that logic never can.

CHAPTER EIGHTEEN
EVERYONE NEEDS A LITTLE SAGACITY
Getting wise principles to live by in their DNA

Sagacity is the ability to make sound judgments. It comes from the word "sage," which means wise one. We all want our children to make wise decisions, to be careful who they associate with, the choices they make, what they say, and how they deal with their possessions. The difficulty is that rarely do these decisions happen naturally. Wisdom or sagacity is required.

There are three primary ways we gain wisdom. One way is by imitation. Do you remember the old W.W.J.D. bracelets many people wore a few years ago? It stood for, "What Would Jesus Do?" It's a statement meant to get us to act wisely as Jesus did. Would Jesus forgive your friend? If yes, well then, so should you. Would Jesus give money to the poor? If yes, then, so should we. Hopefully, our kids learn a great deal of wisdom by imitating us. It doesn't answer every situation but helps our children choose wisely.

The second way we gain wisdom is by reflection. We create scenarios that our children might find themselves in and ask the question, "What's the wisest thing to do?" and follow up their answer by asking, "What can happen if you choose that?" It helps them to evaluate before they get in the situation and to see the series of chain reactions that could result.

The third way is by experience. Either by our own experience or by watching a friend make a mistake and learning from it. When our children make a bad decision, such as not making a good grade, we ask, "How can you avoid making a bad grade next time?"

By the time our children reach first grade, the qualities of being loving, respectful, obedient, self-controlled, grateful, and truthful should be taking root and be evident in their lives. These six core values are the tools we use to help them apply a little sagacity to the different situations they will find themselves in during the training phase of life. Unless you are homeschooling your kids, they will be away from you about as much as they are with you. That means that for much of their day, they won't have you physically with them to help make wise, sagacious choices. They are being influenced by other kids who may not have the same values that you desire. Their coaches and teachers play a role in that influence as well. That can be good, but not always. So, we have to be clear and focused on the issues they will come up against. We also have to be sure we are modeling the values and solutions we want them to grow in. Are you ready?

I always gave my kids short little sayings to remember that, hopefully, would trigger them to think before they acted, and to evaluate where they are in the grand scheme of moving to maturity.

The Choices You Make Today Are the Realities You Live with Tomorrow

Kids are constantly faced with choices. Will I laugh at that joke? Will I stop them from bullying my friend? Will I cheat? Will I be respectful to my teacher? Will I sit with the one no one else wants to sit with? Will I make fun of them? The list goes on and on. Life is relentless when it comes to choices. Even not choosing is making a choice.

When the choice involves people, the golden rule is their greatest friend in giving them advice. Train them to ask this question, "If I was that kid, what would I want someone to do?"

Role play is a great way to help them prepare for those moments. You can do this while riding in the car, during the dinner routine, or just hanging out. Give them a situation and then ask them to give you two to three choices they could make. Then ask them what would happen with each option. It is a powerful way of training your kids to be wise in their decisions.

Temptation and peer pressure will come at them. Temptation comes from our desires. It could be for pride's sake, popularity, or a host of other reasons. While peer-pressure comes from without, the need to belong is what drives it. Hopefully, your "attention and control" efforts are paying off. These also should be role-played. You want them to "feel" the result of their choice. So, during the role play, you might ask the question, "How do you think that will make you feel?" Once emotions are attached to choices, wisdom has a chance to work.

Show Me Your Friends, and I'll Show You Your Future

Friendships have the potential for so much good in our kids' lives. We were never meant to live in isolation. There is a craving deep down in each child that wants attention and belonging. Because of that deep longing, the temptation is to be friends with whoever will feed those longings. So, kids can end up with unhealthy friendships. Friends who don't have the same values that you want for your kids.

We always tried to give our kids a healthy herd of friends. Whether it was our children's ministry at church or team sports, we always tried to steer them toward those kids whose parents shared the same values as we did. Don't underestimate this. We had a few rules. We didn't allow them to go to sleepovers except with cousins and a few select families that we knew well. We've seen the long-term damage done to others during these childhood years from abuse that went unknown to parents.

The golden rule is perfect for friendships as well. We always discouraged tattle-telling unless someone was in danger. Gossiping about anyone, especially a friend, is a quick way to lose them. We didn't allow our kids to say things like, "You're not my friend anymore!" or to put numbers on friendships like, "This is my second-best friend or third-best friend." Don't put a number on friends; just be a valuable friend to those you have.

You Have to Be Able to Order the Pizza

When our kids were small, the only way to get a pizza delivered to our house was to pick up the phone and give them our order. Because I wanted my kids to have good communication skills, we would make our kids order the pizza. They would get so nervous and beg not to have to do it. Now, you may not have that problem with your kids, but it's a great way to get them to learn communication skills.

Beyond the pizza ordering, kids need to know how to "play pitch." We all have that one friend that will dominate the conversation, never giving anyone else a chance to talk. It's what we call, "selfish talk." We taught this to our kids in several ways. I would give the boys a baseball glove, and we would play pitch. I would throw it to them, and they would throw it back, and at some point, I would hold it. They would get a little impatient and then say, "Dad, throw the ball!" I would then use that to explain how it's not any fun to play pitch if someone holds the ball. The same is true in our conversations. If someone asks you a question, answer it, and then ask them a question in return. You could do the same thing by sitting in a circle and tossing a ball around—answer the question that was asked, and then ask a question, and toss the ball to someone else.

Grammar is an integral part of the art of conversation. It may not seem like a big deal, but poor grammar will keep them from opportunities in the future. Their circle of friends may use slang and poor grammar, but they should be able to converse with others using proper language. Reading is the best way to train your children in the use of proper grammar. It helps when you speak correctly as well.

Mind Your Manners

These may seem like silly things to many, but proper manners will give your kids so many advantages. In the south, kids are expected to say, yes ma'am, no ma'am, yes sir, and no sir to adults. It's a sign of respect. Just like opening doors for others, firmly shaking someone's hand, speaking up and not mumbling, and looking people in the eye when they are talking. Keep your finger out of your nose, don't burp, or pass gas. Say please, thank you, and excuse me. These little things make a big impact. Because so few kids do these things today, your child will create an advantage by doing so.

Is This the Wisest Thing to Do?

When it comes to values, this is the one question we tried to instill in each of our kids. It's a simple question with the potential to save a lifetime of grief. Think of what could happen if before kids open their mouth about people, they would ask, "Is this the wisest thing to do?" If they are getting ready to do a crazy stunt, spend hard earned money, or follow the crowd into an adventure, this simple question could keep them from regrets.

These bits of sagacity instilled during this training phase will put your kids well on their way to becoming fit for success in their lives.

CHAPTER NINETEEN
REVERSE ENGINEERING THE TEENAGER
Sketching out what your junior higher will look like

If you're in the middle of parenting kids in this training phase, you have your hands full. I hope it's a rich time for you and that you are aware the kids you are training are not yours to keep. You may not be able to imagine it now, but one day, they will be driving themselves around and won't need your services as their Uber driver any longer. They will be sharing their struggles and hopes with their friends without telling you. They will find a spouse, have some kids of their own, and will be finding their niche and purpose in life. So, we have to make sure that we have prepared them for this life that belongs to them.

If you wrote out your Directional Parenting Blueprint for the discipline phase, then pull it up, and look over it again. You should have placed your child into several scenarios that you might find them in as they begin first grade. You explored behaviors that you wanted them to manifest in their lives. You explored the attitudes that they should have for those behaviors to be present. Lastly, you explored the mindset, those thoughts that create the attitude that produces the behavior that is a reflection of their character. We built all of that around six values. Now, you may have decided on different ones, or you may have more or less than six, but we looked at six values that we wanted to be instilled into our child's life. We wanted them to be loving, respectful, obedient, self-controlled, grateful, and truthful.

After we developed that overall blueprint, we began to break the job down into how we were going to build these into their lives. When building a home from a set of blueprints, you break it down into its parts, like the foundation, the structure, wiring, plumbing, flooring, etc. Using the rhythm of life, you will build the structure for your child in the training phase.

Junior high school years are such a rich transitional time in our lives. We are moving from boys to men and from girls to women. It is, in a real sense, a coming of age time. As parents, we tend to try to hold onto the grade school phase, to maintain control and to protect. You hear your parents' voices saying, "You're always going to be my little girl," (or my little boy). When you envision yours as an adolescent, that same sentiment will creep into your mindset. We have to know what we want them to look like as they reach this twelve-year-old status so that we can train them to be ready for it.

Now, let's update your Directional Parenting Blueprint. Start with envisioning the different scenarios that your child might encounter as they move into junior high. They will be establishing their style of fashion and music, as well as what clique or group they will most identify with. They will be dealing with hormones, feelings, and desires while finding boyfriends and girlfriends. They will be faced with the need to keep up with the newest trends.

Imagine all of that playing itself out in different scenarios and begin to imagine the behavior you want them to display in those junior high years. Those behaviors flow from attitudes— hopefully, attitudes that you have shaped in a healthy way. Those attitudes flow from a mindset (thoughts, principles, and values) that they have embraced.

You might look at these by categories. So, you may look at what they should look like spiritually, physically, mentally, and emotionally. Or, you may break them down into areas like school, sports, home, and friendships. There are many ways to do this. You have to decide what is best for you. The important thing is that you are clear on what you want them to think— what attitudes you want them to possess and then the behavior that houses all those attitudes. How will the wisdom or sagacity that you share with them become a part of their DNA?

All of this is still best formulated during the daily routines. It's time to rethink what those will look like. What can you do during the bedtime routine that will help your child develop the right thinking? Maybe it's in questions, or books, or stories from your time growing up. What will change in the morning routine, and how will you use it. Playtime routine will be replaced with a homework routine. There should still be a quiet time routine as well as the mealtime routine. During these routines, you have the power to shape who your child will become. Take the principles we looked at in the sagacity section and ask yourself how you can build these into your child. Help them learn to make good choices. Help them to evaluate their friendships and how to choose close friends. Help them learn to be an excellent communicator to others, knowing how to have conversations that are beneficial for all. Figure out how to help them become refined in the area of manners and grammar. And get them used to asking themselves, "Is this the wisest thing to do?"

Now, with all of what you want them to become, you should already be honing those qualities yourself. The old, "Do as I say, not as I do," is a terrible mantra. How you live and how you speak to your child will be their inner voice as they move into the next phase of their lives. So, get busy putting that blueprint together.

PART FIVE

DEEPENING RELATIONSHIPS WITH YOUR TEEN IN THE COACHING PHASE

By this phase, your child is moving toward adulthood. Learning how, as parents, to lighten the rules and controls and develop deeper relationships, is crucial. Here, you will learn how this is best achieved as you further help them understand how they develop their body, mind, heart, and soul.

CHAPTER TWENTY

MOVING FROM TRAINING TO COACHING

Putting all that training into practice

In the 1984 version of the classic movie, Karate Kid,[19] Daniel is a struggling youth who finds an odd mentor in an old Oriental man, known as Mr. Miyagi. After seeing Mr. Miyagi destroy several kids who were bullying him, Daniel wants Mr. Miyagi to show him how to fight. The old man gives him a sponge and tells him to wax his car. He tells him to "wax on with the right hand and wax off with the left." Daniel goes through the motions of waxing the car, confused as to why he is doing it. Then, Mr. Miyagi tells him to sand the floor and shows him the specific motion. Again, though frustrated, Daniel does what he's told. Then comes the demand to paint the house. Again, he shows Daniel very specific motions.

After a few weeks of this, Daniel lashes out at the old man, cursing him and telling him that he's tired of being his slave. Mr. Miyagi turns to him, makes him look him in the eye, and demands that he go through each motion. Wax on, wax off. Sand the floor. Paint the house. In the middle of the movements, the old man begins to throw a few punches, and Daniel knocks them all down by instinctively "waxing on and waxing off," or sanding the floor and painting the house. What he thought was nothing more than senseless chores was training him and getting him ready to be coached by Mr. Miyagi in the arena of karate.

It is, hopefully, where you are with your children as they move into the coaching phase of parenting. The time between autumn of the seventh grade and graduation day of senior high school is one of the most transformative times of our children's lives. They are finding their voice, forming opinions, and their bodies are undergoing a metamorphosis of crazy proportions. Socially, they are feeling the pressure to conform to a specific group or clique, and emotionally, they are comparing themselves and evaluating their sense of belonging like never before. If we have trained them in the areas of their values and given them a healthy dose of strategic sagacity, it will bear fruit during this season of their life.

By this time, their personalities are in full bloom. Your lions are roaring, your otters are playfully moving through life, your beaver has set up their rules and guidelines, and your golden retriever is deepening their relationships. They are learning to give and receive love according to the love languages others are using. They have a measure of self-control, and their sagacity is growing. They aren't without flaws, faults, and blemishes; but take a moment and celebrate the good things they do—the heart and mind they are developing. It's time we begin to take the training wheels off and let them feel the balance that they will need to maneuver gracefully and successfully through this season of life.

As in every phase before this one, you will need to change as much as your children. You will need to recognize their growth, spend more time individually with them, talk more. Their days are filled wondering if they measure up; if they have value, are they smart enough, pretty enough, or gifted enough. Now, more than ever, the home has to be a safe place—a place of refuge where they can breathe.

They still need to improve in the area of self-control. They still need PTs (personal time) with you. At least once a day, both of you should toss your phones aside, look each other in the eye, and do a little check-in. Give them your undivided attention for a few minutes to ensure that they see you as a refuge, a safe place.

It's also time to take a look at how to adjust the routines to suit their age. Remember, these routines are where natural training and coaching can take place. The morning routine is a chance to set the tone for the day—to help them learn to be proactive emotionally and to get their head game right. The homework time is a great time to talk about performance, preparation, and how to persevere—all while helping them grow in this area. The mealtime should still be sacred. It might be crowded out by activities where you are eating on the run, but refrain from that if at all possible. And then bedtime will no longer involve you tucking them in or reading a book to them, but it's a great place to reflect on the events of the day and for you to assure them of their worth. You really shouldn't underestimate the value of a healthy check-in and review of the day. They will value it if you aren't trying to push them in a direction they don't want to go. The evening is not the time for those correction discussions.

These years are going to fly by. If you're not careful, you will look back and realize you were merely a spectator instead of being an integral part of their life. Everything you do shouldn't revolve around their activities. Bring them into your world as well.

Take a good look at their behavior. It is the indicator of their emotional state. Behaviors flow from attitudes, and attitudes reflect their emotional quotient. That emotion stems from a belief system that they have embraced. They will need you to continually reinforce a healthy sense of truth into their lives, by your attitudes and behavior as well as by the set of truths you have embraced.

We have to give them more control. I know that's scary, but our goal isn't to keep them safe in the nest. We must teach them to fly and care for themselves. You have to loosen the proverbial leash. Do it now, while you can observe and coach them. Once your child heads to college or moves out on their own, you have less time to observe and coach. Remember, it's okay for them to fail here and there, it's how all of us grow.

CHAPTER TWENTY-ONE
LIFEBOATS, HIDING, AND HURLING
Understanding why we act the way we do

Do you remember what it was like during your junior and senior high school days? No, not the selective memory moments, but the memories that we push to the back of our minds; the ones that were filled with insecurities, fear of not belonging, the fear that others were somehow better than us? Remember those nagging thoughts at the back of our minds and how they affected how we treated others, how we presented ourselves, and in some ways, and how it affected who we truly were? If your child is now in this coaching phase, you will need to revisit those days and those memories.

Several years ago, I was reading the book *Searching for God Knows What* by Donald Miller, the author of *Blue Like Jazz*. In the book, he described an experiment that his teacher gave him when he was in junior high.

I had the same experiment when I was in the eighth grade. We were placed in a circle and told to pretend it was a lifeboat. A bucket was passed around with slips of paper in it and, we each pulled one out. On the paper was written who we were to represent. One was an old person; another was a doctor, a baby, a teacher, and such. We were then to decide as a group who should be thrown overboard because there wasn't room for all of us. I don't remember who we threw overboard, but we were supposed to learn social values. Don Miller referred to it as the "lifeboat theory" and how, if we lived life like we could be tossed overboard, it would explain much of our behavior.

Follow me on this journey. Suppose it's the first day at a new high school, and its lunchtime. You walk into the lunchroom, tray in hand, and begin to look for a place to sit. You see a table filled with people who look like you, but then you spot a table that looks like it would be fun. You try to process whether you think the kids there will like you or not. In essence, you are wondering if they will kick you out of their boat. So, you settle for the safe group—those like you. But once inside the safe group, you begin to find the one who has the power. With this thought of being kicked off the boat in your mind, you subtly avoid the ones who might get thrown off for fear of being associated with them. And you alter your image so that the one in power will like you. See what happens here? It's what life is like if we live in fear that a consensus of peers could get together and decide we didn't have enough value. The fear of not being validated is at the root of what drives peer pressure. In reality, it is what drives much of our negative emotions.

Look at what happens while driving in traffic. Someone gets cut off, or someone slides in ahead of

them when merging. The person feels as though someone invalidated their worth and they get angry, honk
the horn, give a gesture, and tailgate them.

As I began to move in the circles of some influen-
tial people, many would open up to me because I was a
pastor and share their fears, failures, and frustrations.
I learned a valuable lesson from them; the "cool kids"
don't have it all together any more than the rest of us.
Everyone is trying to hold it together. Here is a truth.
Everyone is a fraction of an inch from cracking up! I
drilled this into my kids' heads. I wanted them to know
this truth for several reasons. I didn't want them putting
people on a pedestal, and I didn't want them to see
others as people to be tossed aside. I didn't want them
to be intimidated by those they deemed important, and
I didn't want them to disregard those they would be
tempted to see as unimportant. All of us are a fraction
from cracking up.

If our kids can learn this truth and begin to live in
light of it, it will change their lives. If they see others as
no more important or less important than anyone else,
then peer-pressure is forced to the sidelines. To rightly
see themselves as valuable and of worth and to see others
in the same light will alter the course of their life. They
will become attractional people. They become someone
that others are drawn to for the simple fact that they
won't feel judged by your child. They will feel validated.
And in return, your child will be refreshed as well.

So, where did all of this need for validation and fear
of being thrown off the lifeboat come from? If we travel
back to the beginning, to the Garden of Eden, we can
find our answer. The Bible, in Genesis chapter 3, says
that when God created Adam and Eve, they were "very
good." There is an interesting phrase used at that point.
It says, "They were naked and not ashamed."[36] Now,

when they sinned against God by eating the fruit that He had commanded them not to eat, it says they "saw their nakedness and hid themselves." When God called to them, and they knew that He knew they had sinned, He asked them, "Who told you, you were naked?" Then the finger-pointing began. Adam says, "it was the woman that you gave me!" Then Eve says, "It was the serpent!" We see two characteristics that became true of all of us when sin entered the world. One is that we hide. We seek to cover up our flaws. We wear masks. Look around you, and you will see that this is still going on today. The second characteristic is that we hurl. We assign blame to someone else for our troubles. We point out the flaws in others, their wrongs, their shortcomings. And this too is still going on!

One of the greatest things we can do for our kids is to help them live in light of these truths:

1. Everyone is a fraction of an inch from cracking up.
2. Most people live as though they could be thrown out of the lifeboat.
3. At the core of our being, we try to hide our flaws and hurl blame at others.

Those who recognize their value and that there is room in the lifeboat for everyone will treat people better. Those who know that underneath that confidence or arrogance that people display is someone with insecurities and struggles will see people differently. And those that recognize that human nature is to live life guarded and tend toward playing the victim will be more understanding and patient with others. When we live life treating others in light of these truths, we become a person who will be successful in life. In Proverbs 11:25, Solomon says it like this. "The one who refreshes others will find they are always refreshed themselves."

Of all the things that our kids learned as they were growing up, they remember these sets of truths about the lifeboat. It will make them more confident, less impatient with others, and much freer to express themselves. Get this in them.

CHAPTER TWENTY-TWO
BECOMING YOUR CHILD'S TRUSTED FRIEND
They don't need to be a best friend

The most important thing you can do at this phase of your child's life is to become a trusted friend. I know, I know. The whole world is running around, saying, "I'm not here to be your friend; I'm the parent!" But honestly, that is usually said when we are seeking control over our kids. Our role is not to control our kids; our role is to teach them self-control. When they were in the discipline phase or early in the training phase, we could exercise a little control. But that job was never meant to be long-term. And I recognize that you can say to your child, "My house, my rules! You want to live here; you do as I say." But seriously, let's take a look at a better way.

I learned this with my youngest child. He's fourteen years younger than his next closest sibling. We were riding down our little curvy road one day when he was fifteen years old, and he looked over and said to me, "You know Dad, your one of the best friends I have." As he has gotten a few years older, he has become one of my best friends as well. That is as it should be. Don't fall for the, "I've got to be the tough parent or my kids will think I'm weak and run all over me."

Now, there is a difference between being a trusted friend and trying to be their best friend. Few things are sillier than watching a parent dress like their kids, use slang like their kids, and act childish like their kids. By trusted friend, I mean one that we enjoy spending time with, one who cares enough to say the hard things to us, and one we listen to and respect their opinion. They are safe. These friendships come in all ages, don't they? Some of my most trusted friends are twenty-five years younger, and some are twenty years older. The common link between us is that we love each other, respect each other, and have invested time being with each other. That is what we should all want to be with our kids.

When we are their trusted friend, we can speak into their lives and coach from a position of love, safety, and respect. We aren't in a control situation but an advice and consent role. It is the healthiest and most productive position to be in, to impact our kids for the rest of their lives, long after we are gone. So, let's take a look at some key things we need to develop as parents, to get to that place.

The Ability to Breathe

In these junior and senior high school days, our kids will say things, do things, and wear things that we may not like. Our goal isn't to make them respond to life as we would. Let's avoid the, "shoulda, woulda, coulda" mentality. They are a different personality than you.

We are coaching. While it is true, we are still training them and, in some sense, we are still helping them learn discipline; coaching is our focus. We have to pick and choose our battles much more carefully. If you get in the habit of nagging them about everything they're doing, you will lose the ability to be their trusted friend. No one likes someone hounding them constantly. You don't, and neither do they. There are some boundaries that you have to keep, but these should be obvious. There are certain clothes that reveal too much skin, or that have sayings that are offensive to others. While I'm aware that what we wear will always be offensive to someone, my concern isn't on all the fringe folks that love to be offended, but my thinking is always governed by how my mom, my kids' Memaw, would react to seeing someone wear that. Just because I don't like what they are wearing doesn't mean I have to step in and comment or impose my demands. Breathe!

Our kids will say things we don't like—words and slang and such. Again, I gave it the "Memaw" test. I wanted my kids to be aware of their surroundings. Grammar was something we would correct in private. Proper grammar will help you get much farther down the road of success. I didn't obsess over every use of a cuss word. While we had some zero tolerance words, others we may not have personally used, but we took a breath when they used it. We saved the conversation for another time. My goal is to be a trusted friend, not the speech police. We did, however, make them rephrase negative statements, and we moved them away from gossip. But other than that, we needed to breathe.

Our kids will do certain things we may not like. They may not keep the car or their room as neat as we would. They may like hobbies that make no sense to us and seem a waste of time. Breathe. If it's not hurting anyone and isn't a glaring weakness of character, let it go. Breathe.

They may have a wreck, get a ticket, get suspended, or do something stupid. They will have heartbreaks, failures, struggles, and weaknesses. Breathe. Coach them but breathe. How will you react if your child disappoints you, if your daughter gets pregnant, or your son has sex before marriage? How will you react if they come home high or drunk? We will tend to get angry. That isn't a wrong emotion, but we still need to breathe. Our kids need to know that we love them—that nothing will ever change that. But you have to breathe. Walk them through the situation but breathe. Life is full of highs and lows, brilliant decisions, and monumentally foolish ones. Breathe. Love them, coach them, but breathe.

Listen More, Lecture Less, Ask More Questions

At this age, our kids are getting their voice. They have formed opinions, values, and attitudes. Hopefully, they have been shaped and inspired by you, their parent. But whether they are a mix of yours and the school system's, or their friends' and others', you need to hear their voice. You may still want to be in lecture mode, but you will do so at the risk of losing a healthy relationship with your teen.

Our tendency as parents is to assume that we know what our child is thinking, and instead of listening—really listening to them, we are formulating what "truth" we are going to give them when they finally close their mouth. Our kids want to tell us what's in their heart, mind, and soul, but they want to know they can trust us with it. The best way to do that is to listen well. When they begin talking to you about important issues to them, don't answer right away. Ask them a clarifying question. As you get better at listening and responding, they will see you as someone "safe." A safe person is one in whom we feel comfortable sharing a deeper piece of our story—a deeper piece of what our heart thinks and feels and wants. You may have already figured out the best path for them to take, or the action they should take, but be careful not to give advice too quickly. We are coaching here. Ask questions that will help them forecast and evaluate the different choices, like, "If you choose that option, what do you think could happen?" Once they give that answer, then follow up by saying, "And what will you do then?" or, "Will you like that outcome? Is it best for everyone?"

Improve your interviewing skills by asking questions. Here are a few to get you started: "So, tell me about your life right now? What's going well? What isn't? Concerning friends, ask questions like, "What do you like about your best friend?" How did they get to be your best friend?" Who's the most popular kid in school?" "Why?" "Who feels most left out right now in your school?" In the course of the conversations, you have to talk as well. Not lecture, nor give advice at every turn. You need to be transparent. It will be a game-changer for you and your kids.

Rules - Relationship = Rebellion

As our kids get older, we begin to panic . . . slightly. It seems as though we are losing control and so we have a family meeting, and we declare another rule. Eyes roll, we hear heavy sighs, and resistance begins. You can try giving "one more rule," but it will not have the outcome that you desire. One more rule won't "fix" your kids. Rules don't bring about maturity. Principles and "why" brings maturity.

Here's how it worked in our family. We never had curfews. You know, that arbitrary time when parents demand that their kids be home. At some point, the parents inevitably say, "nothing good ever happens after midnight." We asked them to tell us when they would be home. They would give us an answer, and if their time seemed a little late, we would clarify by asking them why so late. If they gave a legitimate reason, we'd say okay. One thing we demanded was that they would be home a few minutes before the curfew. I told my kids, "Look, if you're a few minutes late, your mom will panic. I will have to call every hospital in the area, hire a private investigator, and it will disrupt my sleep." The real reason we asked that they honor their stated curfew was out of respect for their mom—to keep her from worry. After raising all four kids, we can look back and say we never had a problem in that area, and our kids learned solid principles.

We never grounded our kids at this stage either. Rarely does anything good come from grounding. A simple look at our prison system will tell you that. The punishing stage is over. We have moved on to principles. If you work on being a trusted friend, and you have moved beyond rules, and have built a solid relationship, grounding isn't necessary. You don't do that with your friends or your mate. Stop doing it with your kids.

We always worked hard at this relationship. For trust to grow, your kids need you to apologize to them when you are wrong. They need you to seek their advice about matters where they may be more knowledgeable than you. They need journeys with you, inside jokes with you, emotional stories that you experienced with them. Work on that relationship.

CHAPTER TWENTY-THREE
A LITTLE MORE SAGACITY PLEASE
Help them become wisdom hunters

Wisdom is in short supply in much of the world these days. Those who have wisdom or sagacity stand out, get more out of life, are more attractional, and can influence more people. Sagacity isn't a gift that just happens naturally; it is cultivated by observing others. In the Training Phase section, we said there are three primary ways we gain wisdom. One way is by imitation. Hopefully, our kids learn a great deal of wisdom by imitating us. That puts the pressure on us as parents to step up our game.

The second way is by reflection. We create scenarios that our kids might find themselves in and ask the question, "What's the wisest thing to do?" Then follow up their answer by asking, "What can happen if you choose that?" It helps them evaluate things before they get in the situation, and see the series of events that could result. Another side of reflection is to have a conversation about something that didn't go well and ask, "If you could play that over again, what would you do differently?"

The third way is by experience. Either by our own experience or by watching a friend make a mistake and learning from it. For now, let's look at a few areas where most kids could use a little sagacity.

Stewardship of Your Time, Talent, Temple, Tithe, Testimony

Most people fall into one of two camps when it comes to controlling life. Many play the victim and act like nothing is in their control. Then there are the control freaks who are always trying to control everybody and everything in their lives. I have found that there are five things that we can control in life, and when we manage these areas well, our lives fall into a healthy place.

Time is one of the most valuable treasures we have. It goes in a hurry and never stops. Everyone and everything is begging for our time. Our kids need to learn to guard it and use it wisely. Time is broken down into work or school time, time for reflection and self-evaluation, time for learning, time for fun and relaxation, time for relationships that feed the soul, time for exercise, and time for serving. These are core areas. Finding our rhythm in these areas is vital because if we don't find a routine, silly distractions and time wasters creep in. Social media, video games, and binge-watching TV shows tend to dominate every teen's life. But that is always a choice. Those things should be on the fringe and done in moderation. Have a conversation around these things with your teen.

Each of us has a *talent*. We might call it a passion or a gift, but each of us has been entrusted with an ability to serve the world around us. It may be music or the arts. It could be the ability to encourage or teach. Get your teen to consider what their "verb" is. My verb is refresh. It's what I do. I'm not sure we choose our verb; it's who we are. Serve is my wife, Tammy's verb. Whatever their verb, whatever their talent, it is meant to be practiced, to be used. When we discover what our talent is, we become attractional, alive, and fulfilled.

Our body is considered a *temple*. It houses our soul. It is an amazing creation. It should be cared for with healthy eating, sleeping, and exercise. These can never be ignored. Food is fuel and medicine for our body. A diet filled with fast food or processed food slows the body down. A lack of sleep will keep the body from rejuvenating and replenishing itself. Exercise keeps the body functioning in harmony.

Money has to be guarded. It can slip through our fingers like time. I call this area the *tithe*. Few adults were ever taught how to manage or steward their money. Most of the world in which we live is in debt. Our kids need to be taught to avoid borrowing, to learn how to save up for things they want. Here is a healthy formula for managing money; spend less than you make. When you earn money, give ten percent to ministry, put ten percent away as savings, set five percent aside to give to people in need, five percent for fun, and then the rest is spent on food, rent, gas, etc.

The last treasure that we have is our *testimony*. That is our character—how others see us. It is our reputation. We all have one. If we don't like it, we can change it. Our conversation with our teens has to include helping them determine what principles will drive them. How will others describe them? Will they be seen as a jerk, a snob, or as someone who can't be trusted? Will they be seen as selfish, hard, and ruthless? It is the little things we do, who we are on the inside, that determines our testimony. It is where being a trusted friend to our kids comes in to play. We can speak into them and help them understand how we see them.

Our job as a parent is to coach our teenager in these areas. But you cannot teach what you don't do. So, take a little time and reflect on your own life in these five areas, then have a conversation with your teen.

I look back on my own life and see that certain sayings, principles, and proverbs helped shape who I am, or at least who I strive to be. Our thoughts, what we believe about life, determines our attitudes, and those attitudes are played out in our actions. Here are a few to consider. If you take these and have discussions about these with your kids, you will save them a world of grief.

The Golden Rule is the Only Rule Needed

If we simply treat others as we want to be treated, we will never lack in relationships. Our kids need to know that respect is given, not earned. We give people honor and dignity, no matter their age, their income, or their color. The best advice we can give our kids is this, "If the situation were reversed, how would I want to be treated?"

Life's Not Fair

We tend to compare ourselves to people. If we aren't careful, we will feel like a victim. We are of little value to ourselves and others when we see life from that perspective. We can help our kids learn that everyone's journey is different, and that life is better if we focus on our journey, and not everyone else's.

Readers are Leaders

You can cultivate in your kids a thirst for knowledge and wisdom. I have always watched people transform as they read good books. Novels that make us think about our own life, self-improvement books, poetry, short stories, biographies, all can shape lives for the better.

Show me Your Friends, and I'll Show You Your Future

We become who we hang around. While we are friendly to everyone, we should guard who we choose to get close too. It can't be underestimated.

The Choices you Make Today are the Realities you Live with Tomorrow

Actions always have consequences; always. I wanted my kids to pause for a minute before making a choice and ask, "Is this the wisest thing to do?"

Don't Worry, Be Happy

As Christ-followers, we believe that God is sovereign, that He is in charge, and that He is good, that nothing has come into our lives that wasn't first sifted through His hands. I would say this little phrase to my kids all the time; "We may have lots to think about, but we have nothing to worry about."

You are Good Enough

It is important that our kids realize that they can do anything they want if they are willing to do whatever is necessary to achieve it. Cultivate in your child a "growth mindset." That is one where they truly believe that there is no ceiling on their ability to learn and grow. They are smart enough; they are good enough. If they drift into a "fixed mindset," then they allow what is known as "limiting beliefs" to build barriers to their dreams.

These and so many other little truths should be our focus during this phase. As we become their trusted friend, and we walk through life with them, we give them wisdom. If someone has traveled across the country and sends me information telling me where all the roadblocks are, where the good food is, and where the adventure is, I would want to listen. They have already been where I'm going. In the same way, you are doing that with your kids. You have traveled down the road of life and have seen the pitfalls and dangers, what's important and what isn't. Share that with your kids.

So now, go plot out how you can get a little of this sagacity into your kids' lives. What trips will you take, what places will you visit, how can you give them this wisdom in a way that it will stick?

CHAPTER TWENTY-FOUR
DIRECTIONAL PARENTING BLUEPRINT - COACHING EDITION

Sketching out what your college student will look like

We are in the early stages of getting my mom's house ready to sell. It is now the second time inside of two years that we will update a home to sell it. The first was what we called a mountain home, sitting on five wooded acres. This one is in a little neighborhood in the middle of our little town just outside of Birmingham. You see things differently when you are going to sell your home. That wallpaper in the bathroom may have looked incredible several decades ago, but today, it needs to go. You begin to notice every stain in the carpet, and the leaky faucet that you know exactly how to turn off now has to be replaced. That gate that you don't use because it no longer swings needs some attention. You begin to make a list, and you start prioritizing what to do first. Writing a Directional Parenting Blueprint for the coaching phase of your child is the same process.

At this stage of your parenting, you have history to look back on. You have twelve to eighteen years of history. It's time to evaluate how your child looks "so far," in the area of their thinking, attitudes, and behavior. If you will indulge me one more time, we need to revisit these three areas. Behavior is what everyone sees in our lives and the lives of our kids. *Behavior* is how we act and respond to life as we move through it on our journey. Behavior doesn't happen randomly. It is the result of our attitudes. *Attitude,* while not always readily seen, is where behavior comes from. Attitudes flow from the heart. Behind every act, or behavior, or facial expression, is an attitude of the heart being revealed. Attitudes are the viewpoint, the windshield through which we see this life we are journeying through. There are pessimistic attitudes and optimistic attitudes; selfish attitudes, and selfless attitudes; loving attitudes and hateful attitudes; risky or cautious, capitalist or socialist, unifying or dividing. Attitudes flow from a healthy self-esteem or from an unhealthy self-esteem; a generous attitude or a hoarding attitude. Now, these attitudes come from somewhere. They didn't just randomly appear. If we can shape the attitude, we can alter the behavior.

Attitudes flow from the heart. The heart is always thinking and always desiring. The heart is shaped by what we think. *Thought* is the brain processing a set of truths. As we said earlier in this book, not all truths we believe are, in fact, true. Not all the thoughts we hold are accurate. Remember our conversation about the concept of fairness? We crave that others will be fair to us. We are less concerned that we are fair to others, but that is human nature. Our heart has this thought about fairness running in the background of our mind so that when we are treated in what we perceive to be an unfair act, our attitude processes that scene, it desires fairness, and our behavior screams out, "No Fair!" We all know that life isn't fair. But until we know that instinctively, we will always react to unfairness in a victim-like, selfish way.

Truth matters. Truth is tricky. We can all be deceived about what is true and what isn't. Just because life should be fair, it doesn't mean that it is. Solomon says, "As a person thinks in their heart, so are they." If we can direct the thoughts of our kids, we can shape their attitudes, which will alter their behavior. So, now more than at any phase of raising kids, a close look at the truths our kid will hold when they move to adulthood is crucial to how they will live out their lives. It's why we are careful in choosing who teaches, coaches, or oversees our kids as they are growing up. It's one of the reasons that I have always created little sayings that become principles to govern my life and those I'm privileged to influence. Truth matters. It matters because it shapes our attitudes. Attitudes matter because they shape our behavior. Behavior matters because it defines our character, our reputation, and who we are.

If you have a child in the *Coaching Phase*, I want you to imagine what they will look like as they head off to college or begin their life beyond high school. Again, some of the questions will be similar to the other phases, but with a deeper layer. What kind of driver will they be? How will their bosses see them as they begin work? Will they have an upbeat, positive view of life? Will they be fierce or fearful? Will they be able to change a flat tire or jump a car off? Will they be loving? Gracious? Humble? Will exude confidence that attracts others? How will they respond when the core values they hold are attacked as out of date or wrong and silly? Will they be able to bounce back from a broken heart? How will they handle betrayal?

As you begin to explore these areas, you are going to realize that what you're doing is shaping their values. Your kids will tend to inherit your values. What you may discover as you go through this process is that *your* values need shifting as well. So, as we have stated a few times already, you will most likely change as much as your kids. As parents, we are in the change business. It begins with feeding and filling our child's brain with truth, philosophies, and principles. So, get a journal, find a creative spot, and start adding to your "Directional Parenting Blueprint" for this phase of your child's life.

In the discipline phase, we looked at six values that we wanted to instill into our child's life. We wanted them to be loving, respectful, obedient, self-controlled, grateful, and truthful.

In the training phase, we took a look at what we wanted them to look like spiritually, physically, mentally, and emotionally. That was just one way to write out the blueprint. You decided what was best for you. The important thing is that you were clear on what you wanted them to think, what attitudes you wanted them to possess, and then the behavior that houses all those attitudes; and we built this around the daily routines.

Now, as we write out this final Directional Parenting Blueprint for the coaching phase, we are envisioning our babies, our kids, our adolescent as an adult. Crazy thought right, but it's crucial that we take an in-depth, well thought out, look at how we envision them to be. What values will they have? What principles will they hold unswervingly to? How will they behave when life hits them hard? When life throws them a curve? When they acquire success? What core truths will they die for? It's now time to figure out, specifically, what those things are and how you will plant them deep into your child's DNA.

Take a look at the "lifeboat theory" and create ways in which you will teach them their values, where they come from, and the value that all people bring. Look back over the sagacity chapter and brainstorm how you can best implement the principles into your kid's life. Create some of your own sagacity principles. What you are doing is creating a "life curriculum" as your child moves into adulthood. Write it down. Read it to them. Put it into practice in your own life. Start putting the blueprint into practice for them.

I'm excited for you as you enjoy these days of raising your children to be kids who turn out right. Breathe in every second. It's a cliché, I know, but it's true. These years will fly by. Don't rush them, savor them. I can't wait to hear your stories of how you and your kids are doing.

EPILOGUE
LEAVING THE LIGHT ON!

I finished writing the last chapter of this book twenty days after my eighty-nine-year-old mother passed away. Tammy, my youngest son Jackson, and I had moved in with her seven months earlier and cared for her during the last season of her life on earth. In truth, you never get rid of your kids. My mom loved us being there. We loved being there. My mom and dad always "left the light on." They made it easy for their kids to come home, whether it was for a meal, a weekend, or an extended stay.

I look back over my life and realize how fast my childhood was, and how fast my kids grew up. We weren't ready for them to leave when the time came. We prepared them for that day. It is inevitable that one day, your kids will head out on their own too. But if we have done our job, there will always be a craving within them to come home.

We have a light that sits on our library table near our front door. It's on every night. When Jackson comes in, no matter how late, he turns it off. If we get up at night and the light is off, we know he's home. That light serves as a reminder, not just to him, but to all the kids, that they are always welcome.

We've tried to create an environment where they knew they were welcome. First, we made it a safe place. Home should be the safest place on earth. Cultivate that. Let forgiveness and patience flow freely. Secondly, be their biggest fan. Keep up with what's happening in their world. Give them a call or text. And thirdly, create special times of gathering away from the holiday season. Have your own mini-reunion. Find things to celebrate and gather them up. We retreat to the mountains in the fall, and we gather at the beach in late spring.

Guard your family. Celebrate them. Love them. Be gracious to them . . . and you may just look back on your life and realize you raised kids who turned out right!

ENDNOTES

1   Andy Stanley, "The Principle of the Path: How to Get from Where You Are to Where You Want to Be," Thomas Nelson, March 2009

2   Romans 8:28 NIV

3   Acts 17:26 NIV

4   Proverbs 23:7 KJV

5   Psalm 139:13 NIV

6   Psalm 127:3 NLT

7   Proverbs 22:6 KJV

8   John Trent, "The Treasure Tree: Helping Kids Understand Their Personality." March 1998

9   Proverbs 19:18 ESV

10 Proverbs 22:15 ESV

11 Proverbs 29:15 ESV

12 Proverbs 29:17 ESV

13   Paul David Tripp. Parenting: 14 Gospel Principles That Can Radically Change Your Family. September 2016

14   Proverbs 4:23 NIV

15   William H. McRaven. Make Your Bed: Little Things That Can Change Your Life... And Maybe Your World. Grand Central Publishing. April 2017

16   Galatians 6:9 NLT

17   Ecclesiastes 8:15 ESV

18   Gary Chapman. The 5 Love Languages. Northfield Publishing. January 2015

19   Robert Mark Kamen. *Karate Kid*. Directed by John G. Avildsen. 1984

ABOUT THE AUTHOR

Randy has a passion to refresh others. He believes life is an incredible journey filled with passions, hopes, wonders, and relationships. In the midst of this, life can be a struggle. Randy has a natural ability, forged in the fires and trials of life, to give fresh hope to others in the areas of family, relationships, life, and soul.

Randy is a Visioneer with a God-given talent to help others envision a better future. He is able to see where they are in their journey and then, by applying uncommon common sense, takes the difficult areas of relationships and life and breaks them down into their most simple form. It is with that understanding that he leads others to creating a blueprint that will get them to a better place.

He and his wife, Tammy, have been blessed with four incredible children and nine grandchildren at this point in life. Birmingham Alabama is their home.

Previous Writing:

Randy Pardue has been speaking to audiences for over thirty-five years. He is a teller of stories with a purpose. Under his pen name, "Uncle Poppy," he has authored two children's books: *Sandy the Selfish Seagull* (2016) and, *A Blue Chair Christmas* (2015).

Randy has been interviewed on shows such as *Roxanne & Friends* on 93.7 WDJC in Birmingham, and *News at Noon* on WBRC Fox 6 in Birmingham. He has spoken to schools, PTAs, and libraries all across Alabama, sharing stories and reading portions of his children's books.

He teaches workshops on marriage and family in the USA as well as internationally in Europe, Asia, and Central America. He has taught as an adjunct professor at Mission India Theological Seminary.

He teaches and consults with businesses on leadership, processes and procedures, as well as stress management.

He is one of the teaching pastors at Restoration Gathering in Birmingham, AL.

CPSIA information can be obtained
at www.ICGtesting.com
Printed in the USA
LVHW011230260819
628923LV00008B/102/P

9 781640 853553